Gary —

To one great guy I've had the privilege to meet and work with.

Hope you enjoy.

Ron

MARKETING SURVIVAL IN A DIGITAL WORLD

RON MARSHALL

Big RAM Publishing LLC

Copyright © 2013 by Ron A. Marshall

All rights reserved. This book or any portion thereof
may not be reproduced or used in any manner whatsoever
without the express written permission of the publisher
except for the use of brief quotations in a book review.

Printed in the United States of America
First Printing, 2013
ISBN **978-0-9898559-0-7**
Big RAM Publishing LLC
1320 North Stewart Avenue
Springfield, MO 65802

ACKNOWLEDGEMENTS

I would like to thank the many clients, business associates, employees and teachers who have contributed to the experiences and lessons outlined in this book.

A special thanks to my daughter Heather, who tirelessly corrected my creative approach to spelling and grammar.

Most of all, thanks to my wife Patty for her endless support and unconditional love.

Table of Contents

INTRODUCTION 9

CHAPTER 1: MARKETING OVERVIEW 13
    When Advertising Was Enough 13
    A.I.E.A.A. - The Buying Processes 14
    The Decline of Advertising 16
    You're More Replaceable Now 19
    Advertising Can't Fix You 23

CHAPTER 2: BRANDING 31
    Branding Characteristics.. 31
    Branding Advantages 35
    Unique Sales Proposition (USP).. 40
    Building Your Brand 51

CHAPTER 3: RESEARCH 53
    Quantitative Reports 54
    Qualitative Research... 55
    Market Demand 57
    Competitive Research.. 59
    Customer Profiling 61

CHAPTER 4: ADVERTISING 71
    Advertising Budget.. 73
    Forecasting 76
    Traditional Media 81
    Direct Marketing... 85

When Should You Advertise?.. 94
Pre-Placement Evaluation 104
Media placement 114

CHAPTER 5: WEBSITES 119
Website MCD 120
What Your Website Must Do.. 122
As Important As Your Store 122
Website Design and Development 122

CHAPTER 6: SEARCH ENGINE MARKETING 125
Position is Important 125
Most Keyword Searches Are By Product 127
Dynamic Search 127
SEM Components 128
SEO - Search Engine Optimization... 129
Online Advertising... 134
Social Media 137

CHAPTER 7: PUBLIC RELATIONS 143

CHAPTER 8: PLANNING 145
Business/Marketing Planning Software 145
Task and Timeline Tracking Programs 146
Project-Level Collaboration Programs... 146
Keeping Track of the Plan.. 147

CHAPTER 9: POST-PLACEMENT EVALUATION............................ 149
External and Internal Performance Factors................................... 150
Isolate Your Media for Measurement 152
Sourcing the Cause.. 152
You Must Continually Test... 153
Measurement Is Not Without Flaws 153
Technology Makes It Easier To Measure 155

CHAPTER 10: MARKETING & ADVERTISING AGENCIES 159

CONCLUSION.. 163

INTRODUCTION

Does it seem like it's harder to get customers these days? Do you find yourself searching for solutions, trying different advertising media, adding new online components, yet nothing seems to make much difference? If so, you're not alone.

Times are tough on businesses and will probably continue to be. We are evolving into a world economy where your competition is no longer limited to the store down the street. Now every similar business in town is a competitor for your market share; maybe even those in other states and countries.

The traditional advertising you relied on in the past will never work as well again. With audiences fragmenting across a plethora of different media and social communications, you can't rely on one or two forms of advertising to reach most of them anymore.

On the other hand, this doesn't mean mass media cannot still play an effective role in your marketing programs. Since digital has arrived, too many people are abandoning hard-earned and effective positioning created by mass media and re-directing their attention solely to online social efforts.

Marketing Survival means to gain an understanding of how both traditional and digital marketing work, and how they can work together to achieve good results. For your business to prosper, you're going to need a broader understand than was required in the past.

The purpose of this book is to offer good, fundamental advice to help you succeed in today's complex and competitive marketing environment. The content includes information obtained from research, as well as successes and mistakes I've observed (and made) while working with many forms of advertising and marketing applications over 30 years.

In this book you'll learn:

1. The core reasons why the rules of marketing and advertising have changed so quickly.
2. Why you need to transform your company, services or products into a valued brand.
3. The most important marketing components you need in your arsenal; how to use them and how to evaluate their effectiveness.

The Outline

The first section of this book is an overview of the process people use to make buying decisions, and how new technology has replaced advertising's role in that process. I also explain how the Internet has empowered buyers and has created a very exposed position for businesses that are not truly competitive.

The next section addresses why it's important for businesses to focus on building a valued Brand, not just through communications, but from within their organization. I'll provide some advice on how to create and build Unique Sales Propositions (USP) that resonate with buyers, and how they help position your service or product as a benefit to your consumers.

Marketing Overview

The final sections explain fundamental marketing components such as research, traditional advertising, online marketing, media buying, budgeting and planning. Most of you will not need everything I've listed, but for those of you who do, these sections will help you understand how you should use them, and will also be handy as a reference manual.

There is much to cover. Let's get started.

1

MARKETING OVERVIEW

When Advertising Was Enough

According to Wikipedia—*"Marketing is the process of communicating the value of a product or service to customers, for the purpose of selling the product or service. It is a critical business function for attracting customers."*

As implied here, most people think of marketing as simply a communication tool. Most folks even use the terms marketing and advertising interchangeably. For the record, advertising is merely a component of marketing, and marketing is not simply a communication function.

In fact, marketing has many components; research, planning, pricing, public relations, etc. In the past, however, advertising was enough for most small and mid-sized businesses. Advertising was the sturdy and reliable net woven out of creativity that business used to harvest buyers. Through advertising, the public was told what was cool and what wasn't. Attractive models or confident spokespersons authoritatively stated why their products were necessary, and we believed! Jingles, catchy slogans or icons produced noticeable, entertaining and compelling advertisements we'd sing and quote. Products' reputations were built on the quality of their commercials and campaigns and not always for what they actually delivered. It was part of our culture.

Best of all, everybody could be reached through only a few media channels: television, radio, newspapers, magazines and billboards. The public was literally a "captured audience" due to limited entertainment options. Advertisers or their agencies simply selected one or two media and placed their advertising orders. If the offer was good and demand existed, they'd often see a lift in sales.

Advertising was in control. This was because advertising could generally produce three responses from the public: Awareness, Interest and Evaluation.

A.I.E.A.A. - The Buying Processes

A.I.E.A.A. is a simple model of the mental and emotional process people go through, which eventually leads to selecting a product or service. (The industry description of this process is usually referred to as A.I.D.A.: Awareness, Interest, Desire and Action. I modified the process to A.I.E.A.A. because I think it gives a more accurate picture of the buying process.)

A.I.E.A.A. includes five phases:

1. **Awareness**—*"What is this?"* A prospect must first become aware a product or service exists before they can buy it.
2. **Interest**—*"There's that widget thing again. What does it do?"* The more people see an offer that may be relevant to them, the more they pay attention.
3. **Evaluation**—*"I may want a widget. I'm going to check it out a little more."* The more people pay attention to an offer, the more they learn about it and evaluate it.

4. **Acceptance**—*"I want a widget and I can justify the cost."* Every sale requires the prospect to accept that the product or service has value to them.
5. **Action**—*"I'm going to go buy that widget today."* The prospect has made the decision to act and purchase the product or service.

We all go through these steps before we buy anything from peanut butter to penthouses. Sound over-simplified? Test yourself. When you considered any of the following, think about the five phases and see if all apply.

- Buying a car
- Hiring a plumber
- Deciding where to have dinner
- Choosing a mate

Even an impulse buy goes through these five steps, only it occurs much faster and more subconsciously.

Advertising's Primary Job

Before the Internet, advertising could effectively push prospects through the first three steps of the buying process and sales would normally follow (more or less, to some degree):

1. **Awareness:** Media choices were few, and there were no other distractions
2. **Interest:** Our clever creativity aroused their curiosity
3. **Evaluation:** The evaluation was based on the "salesmanship" of the advertisement and the "credibility" of being on TV. There really wasn't any other way to investigate or compare available, so we assumed most advertising claims were true. (We *were so naïve.*)

The Decline of Advertising

Up until the last couple of decades, advertising has been our primary source to learn about the introduction of new products and services. As I explained, it has been a primary influence on our perceptions and opinions, and had the power to convince us what to believe.

While advertising is certainly not dead, today it is far less effective and influential. Its ability to reach as many people to create Awareness has been reduced to a fraction of what it was due to increasing Audience Fragmentation, Advertising Volume and Online Distraction.

Audience Fragmentation

Around 1995 media options really started to expand. We went from a few local television stations to over 400 stations through cable. Niche magazine publications grew, and the number of radio stations increased. The added choices made it more difficult and more expensive to reach your buyers. You simply couldn't afford to advertise everywhere.

The fragmenting of the audience reduced the effectiveness of traditional media staples.

- The Audit Bureau of Circulations (ABC) reported daily newspaper print readership has fallen 22.5 percent, and Sunday has fallen almost 28 percent in just the last five years.
- Successful network television prime time shows used to capture around 33 percent of adults. In the 70's, *M.A.S.H.* carried almost 45 percent every week. By 2005, *Desperate Housewives* was considered a huge rating success, yet it only averaged 14 percent of the adult population as an audience. As you might guess, its' far less than that today.

The means of how people become aware of you has shifted radically. According to a report dated July 30, 2013 by MarketingCharts.com, audiences are most likely to learn about new product and brands from TV

Marketing Overview

(58%), friends and family (54%), and on the Internet (54%). The results differ significantly when sorting by age bracket. In the 18-34 age group, the Internet is the primary source of discovery (59%), friends and family (56%) with TV falling to third (48%).

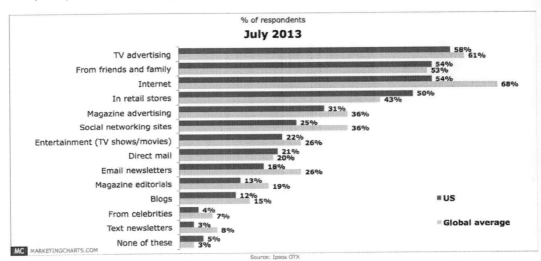

Advertising Volume

When you create more media channels you'll create more advertising. Today Americans (and most modernized countries) are bombarded with advertisements. I'm talking about a tsunami of commercials, print ads, brand labels or anything a business can produce to get your attention and compel you to buy. Marketing experts estimate that most Americans are exposed to around 4,000 to 10,000 advertisements each day.

Like many, I thought that number sounded a little far-fetched. So I actually decided to dedicate one entire day to test it myself. I asked my wife and anyone I thought I would come in contact with to not distract me too much. I wanted to pay keen attention to the direct and indirect advertising impressions I was exposed to.

On my test day, I woke up in the morning to my Sony radio-alarm clock, heard about 14 ads on KTTS before I opened my eyes and hit the snooze on my Sony clock. I used my Panasonic TV and Dish Network receiver remotes, noticed a Kenwood receiver and Toshiba DVD player, and watched/listened to 46 TV commercials as I got going.

Standing at my sink I turned on my Moen faucet, grabbed my Crest toothbrush and Pearl Drops toothpaste, my Mennen shaving cream, my Schick razor and Right Guard deodorant. I count 51 product labels within eyesight in my medicine cabinet and 47 other labels just standing in our bathroom while looking around. I'm up to around 200 ads and my hair isn't even combed yet.

I got dressed in my Fruit of the Loom undershirt, Big Dog shirt, Wrangler Jeans and Nike shoes; 11 brand advertisements are within eyesight in the closet. I'm not digging for them.

I opened my pantry and counted 214 food brand labels, all colorful and professionally created. I get my box of Kellogg's for my Hiland Dairy milk and count 62 product brands. I open a can of Folgers coffee to brew in my Mr. Coffee maker. I've gotten around 487 ad exposures and I haven't even finished breakfast.

I ended my experiment here. I was brand-weary and knew the exposures would become even more frequent when I stepped out my front door. I concluded that they were probably telling the truth.

Of course, most people won't actually recall seeing 10,000 messages. This is because in order to keep our sanity, we've developed a screening process to ignore most advertising messages. Less than 100 of them make it past our "attention wall" each day. It's simply a matter of self-preservation.

Online Distraction

As quickly as advertising has declined, new marketing communication technology has emerged and created a distraction like nothing we have ever experienced. New "communication components" such as websites, Facebook, Netflix, streaming video, etc. have entered the arena and have changed our lifestyles as well as the way we research and make buying decisions.

Surfing became popular as we were dazzled by this newfound electronic library. Consequently, the more time consumers spend online, the less time they spent in front of the televisions, or reading magazines and newspapers.

Evaluation Moved Online

Naturally, as advertising's ability to generate Awareness declined so did it's ability to push people into Interest. As online grew it created a *disruption in the A.I.E.A.A. process.* As Websites began popping up, consumers started using these to research, investigate and Evaluate.

People no longer put much stock in the claims made in TV commercial or magazine ads. While it may spark interest, people go online to research, look for reviews, and compare similar competitors to see if there is a better deal. And this has led to what I call "The Big S"— Substitution.

You're More Replaceable Now

I think the most serious problem companies now face is how easily buyers can find competitors, and then compare and replace them in favor of a more appealing competitor. The Internet has made your product, business or services more replaceable than ever before.

Marketing Survival in a Digital World

In the past, consumer shopping options were usually limited to businesses that:

- They could physically see
- Someone told them about
- Reached them through advertising or
- They found listed in the yellow pages

Regarding a business or product's reputation, a consumer's only source was generally limited to what they heard from friends, family or through the Better Business Bureau.

Today consumers can easily find any number of business, products and services online, and can just as easily compare them all, side-by-side. Unless there is something of distinct value that sets one business over the others, the purchase will probably be awarded to the business with the lowest price.

Even the great established brands have found they are prey to easy substitution due to a lack of differentiating value from online competitors. In 2013 alone, companies like Best Buy, JC Penny's, Barnes and Noble, Sears, Kmart, Radio Shack, and several others announced they would be closing 17 percent to 34 percent of their brick and mortar stores due to sales lost to online competitors. Many cited Amazon as one of their single most ferocious rivals.

The battlefield is no longer within a few blocks or even within a town. Online has changed the rules and those who cannot embrace it, will not long compete.

Yesterday:

- **You were convenient.** You were located closer to your primary buyers. If you offered what they were looking for, they didn't have much motivation to drive farther.
- **Buyers were more ignorant.** If a competitor's advertising or word-of-mouth couldn't convince buyers they offered better value

Marketing Overview

or quality, or significantly lower prices, people tended to believe you were as good as any and stayed put. They simply lacked the awareness of better options, as well as the ability to research.

Today:

- **Convenience doesn't matter as much.** You've lost most of the convenience benefit. Now, people can order what they want online. They don't even have to leave the house to go shopping.
- **Their eyes have been opened.** You've lost the advantage of ignorance. Buyers can find virtually anything they want online. They can research an almost unlimited number of competitors that offer what you do. They can check your reputation in just a few minutes.
- **They can line you up side-by-side and compare.** With all this information, they can easily compare you to your competitors. Unless you really and truly have something that is more valuable or relevant to them, it will come down to the lowest price. A bidding war.
- **The big stores can outbid you.** More packaged goods are being controlled and distributed by larger companies, who have more marketing assets and larger budgets. You will not be able to undercut their prices.
- **The audience continues to fragment.** You now have to have your marketing or advertising in more places, i.e. on websites, on Facebook, in blogs,
- **Your reputation is now under a public microscope.** Thanks to online, your reputation is more important now than ever before. Eighty percent of prospects will not investigate a business with bad online reviews when other options are available.

The Consumer Has Control

If it feels like we are not in control anymore, it's because we're not. The consumer is. And that has brought a change in their attitudes as well. Buyers are no longer happy just being wide receivers. These days they want to play quarterback. They want to be in charge, and now they're empowered to demand it.

The shift to buyer-controlled marketing isn't a new lesson. The Japanese did it to the American auto industry back in the 1980's. For decades, Detroit created cars and said "Come and get them!" They didn't care what the consumer wanted. Henry Ford said "They can have any color (car) they want as long as it's black."

The Japanese had the audacity to go to the buyers and asked: "What type of car may I build for you?" We all know how that turned out. The Japanese automakers buried the American manufacturers and have never slowed down. They continue to master the process of asking what people want and then producing it for them, and at a lower price. Additionally, the Japanese raised the bar on quality. Japanese cars quickly gained a reputation for quality and reliability. American cars were slow to catch up.

Now, the Internet is doing the same thing to all other businesses and manufacturers. It has provided a world-wide buyer's forum wherein, if you don't listen to them and deliver want they want at a competitive price, somebody else will. If you don't deliver high value and quality, everybody's going to know about it, and your market share will decline.

Steven Jobs said, "You've got to start with the customer experience and work back toward the technology—not the other way around." He understood the danger of blindly deciding what the public wants or needs. He grew one of the most successful brands in the world by staying ahead of the curve, always, always asking for the consumer's input.

Change is the new norm. Consumer opinions and purchasing options are changing at break-neck speed, compared to just a few years ago. It's important to understand that this will continue. There will be no place to settle-in and get comfortable down the road. To play the game, you've got to stay in the game.

Advertising Can't Fix You

Depending on advertising to overcome a business or product flaw will lead you to disaster. It is a very weak and expensive crutch. Spending good money advertising a poorly run company is like the old saying: "You can't make a silk purse out of a sow's ear."

A study of 20,000 consumers published by McKinsey Quarterly revealed when considering an automobile purchase, company-driven marketing only effected consumer consideration by 39 percent. In other categories it was generally lower. The bulk of the decision was based on word of mouth, online research and/or past experience.

Good marketing starts from the inside with a rigid and unbiased examination, regular re-examinations of your quality, your products, your service, and your competition. You must strive to be excellent at everything you claim to be.

Why? Because when the promise of value as described in the advertising is not delivered by the company, even great investments in advertising and marketing will not sustain it for very long. Time and again, I've seen companies invest more into "cover-up" advertising than it would have cost to correct what they were trying to cover-up.

The Odds Are Tough

Although not impossible, continuing to generate enough business primarily through marketing communications is a tough proposition. Various studies have shown 50 to 85 percent of advertising *has no effect on sales*.

Professor Gerard Tellis and his associates from the USC Marshall School of Business summarized the findings from hundreds of prior studies on advertising through a method called "meta-analysis." Here are two of their conclusions:

The effect of advertising is quite small. A 1 percent increase in advertising expenditures leads to .1 percent increase in sales or market share. In other words, the sales return to advertising is 1/10th of its input in terms of expenditures.

About half of all ads are ineffective. This result represents a large fraction of ineffectiveness. It may be because firms continue campaigns past their period of effectiveness, persist with ineffective ads, or just fail to test if their ads work.

You may say: *"Why even try to advertise? The odds are against me!"* This is true. The odds are against you *if you don't provide genuine value and quality*. It's still a good strategy if you deliver what people want and you *retain* them.

Unique Offerings

There are many businesses that have a direct and measurable gain from their advertising. They shut it off, sales slowdown or stop. Turn it on, customers come back. These types of businesses typically have a higher return than the 1/10 example given previously. This is normally unfulfilled demand without much competition. Simply creating the Awareness through advertising can deliver an acceptable return to the expense because it is unique.

Let's now assume your product or service has demand but is not unique, and has competitors who also advertise. Both of these factors

Marketing Overview

would tend to drive your advertising ROI down toward the lower 1/10 average. In these cases, would it still make sense to advertise?

Probably. If there is demand for a product, and all other things being equal, the business that promotes itself through advertising will certainly gain the advantage over the other who does not. So your advertising often acts more as self-defense, and the advertising yields less than for other businesses.

Again, where you really gain the upper hand is if you're better at retaining customers and earning repeat business. Over time you can recoup your initial advertising expense, provided you hold onto the customers.

Marketing Priorities

When a company owner or manager asks me what their marketing should focus on, I usually state these four objectives, in order of priority:

1. Retain your customers
2. Grow incremental sales from your customers
3. Get referrals from your customers
4. Go after new customers

Although these may seem oversimplified, the fundamental principle of applying your marketing to hold on to what you have earned sets the stage for longevity and growth in the greatest companies that exist. Unbelievably, most small- to mid-sized companies tend to ignore the first three and focus primarily on the forth step: gaining new business. Most flat out refuse to survey for customer satisfaction.

The beginning of a relationship with a new customer is often the least profitable stage in the relationship. You might have to invest thousands in media to make prospects aware that you exist. In more competitive environments, you may also have to offer loss-leader discounts to compel new prospects to sample your offerings, in hopes they'll come back in the future and buy at normal prices, wherein you can re-coup your initial investments. If they don't like what you offer the first time, they won't come back and you'll be stuck trying to cover overhead and cost of goods on very thin margins.

Statistically, it costs an average of 1/10 as much to retain customers as it does to acquire new ones, so you might see why I think these are very practical objectives to always strive for.

I'm not saying that retention alone will be enough. Customers churn over time, and you must replace those that do. And more customers usually mean growth. What I am saying is that keeping a consistent focus on customer retention will force you to improve, and will remind you not to assume they will continue to return regardless of your quality or service.

The more you improve your quality, the better your marketing and advertising will meet your expectations. Here is a good objective every business owner should try to achieve:

"Do everything you can to create a business that does not need marketing or advertising to survive and profit."

Get in the Habit of Regular Tune-Ups

Regularly re-examine your business and offers:

- Have you done enough research to determine that there is sufficient market demand for your product or service?
- Are you certain you're competitively priced, or offer the same or better value than your competitors?
- Have you considered that you could have internal issues that will counter-act your advertising or marketing efforts?

How often do you stop and take another look at your business from the position of a prospect on their first visit to your store?

- Is your appearance right?
- Is your staff knowledgeable and friendly?
- Can they sell?

Marketing Overview

- Is your product or service mix or inventories correct?

Get Out of Denial

I often need to have a frank discussion with prospective or existing clients regarding operational issues that have a negative effect on customer satisfaction. In almost every case they never, ever want to hear it. Most will politely acknowledge my position and sincerely appreciate the feedback. Yet too often, they never really change.

Those who don't hold on to the unrealistic expectation that their marketing or advertising will fix the problems, cover them up, blind and dazzle the public so they don't notice poor service or quality, etc. When it does not and their sales tank, the advertising or agency becomes the scapegoat.

I recently sat down to meet with a client we've had for a few years. When we first met, he said his restaurant had about three months left to live if we couldn't bring in business. Fortunately, we were able to develop and launch an extremely successful advertising campaign with a crazy jingle that made his restaurant a household name in his market area. His business surged and he was very happy.

Flash forward six months. The same client is sitting in my office telling me business is down again, and he needs the advertising improved to bring people into the restaurant like before. I could have simply suggested some new advertising production or different media, but instead I challenged him. I asked him if he knew *"why"* his business was down. He had no idea. The product was still great—the best in town.

I actually knew the problem. The client had a very high "churn" rate. This is when you lose customers and have to replace them with new customers. When I told him I believed the problem stemmed from the combination of his offbeat décor, somewhat obscure location, and high prices (as the Great Recession was in full swing), he didn't believe me.

To prove it I decided to tell him about an experience I had a few weeks earlier when I had made plans to take my wife and some friends to the client's restaurant for dinner. As we all climbed into the car, our friends asked us if we would mind going somewhere else.

Although his restaurant was perceived as very pricey, this was not the reason they changed their mind. The main reason, according to the ladies in the group was, *"the ambiance was OK for lunch, but if we're going to spend that much money we want to go someplace a little nicer."* One cited the fact that a roll of paper towels sitting on the table worked good for a burger joint, but not for an expensive dinner date.

My client was a bit uncomfortable as I further explained *"Your problem is really not your advertising. We've created mass Awareness and Interest; everybody in town can sing your jingle. You've had a huge volume of new customers come in and give your restaurant a try. They all love your food but they just don't come back because your prices are high and the ambiance doesn't support the experience for that type of expense. Make some changes internally and you'll fix the problem."*

A few days later, the client asked us to send an email survey to 1000 of his customers we had in his database, to determine what *they* thought. You can probably guess what the vast majority of the responses concluded—the same thing we'd all been telling him.

He finally made some of the recommended changes, but unfortunately several months too late. By that time public opinion was set. We just couldn't bring them back in with marketing as fast as internal issues lost them.

And another

We had another client with a home improvement store. We had helped him build a great brand supported by a strong and catchy advertising campaign that delivered plenty of qualified prospects for many years.

He then opened a new store where the only entrance was in the back, in an area enclosed by chain link fencing. It gave the impression you were entering a delivery or contractor-only area.

Naturally, sales never took off and naturally the client blamed the advertising. When I tried to bring the client attention to entrance problem, he didn't buy it. Even after I told him that I'd personally observed customers drive in and immediately drive back out (because there were no signs telling them where they were supposed to come in), he didn't want to change it: *"Be too expensive,"* he said.

As a result, he never corrected the problem and he was eventually forced to close the store, which was so devastating it took down his other location as well. If this one thing had been corrected, it could be an entirely different ending.

And another

Another client invested a ton of money in advertising, but the Year-Over-Year (YOY) sales were still declining. This was a bridal store, where the experience of the purchase is as important as the product. Research revealed that although they were the best-known, independent bridal shop, they also had the lowest loyalty of all independents. We had personally witnessed bad service in the store, and had many other first-hand accounts validating the same. Still, the client didn't believe it and placed the blame on the advertising.

Eventually secret shoppers provided the proof. Unfortunately, his reluctance and delay to address the core issue (operations) created long-lasting reputation issues that were very difficult and expensive to overcome.

These are not isolated cases. All businesses have operational or personnel problems which reduce their ability to deliver quality and/or service to clients. Too often they will minimize it, deny it or ignore it, and blame their marketing instead of tackling the problem inside.

You Need to Get Exceptional

If this sounds ominous, that's good. That is what I intended.

Online has stripped businesses of the advantages of buyer ignorance and proximity to which they had become so accustomed. Marketers cannot deliver the sales or the market share of the past by simply being creative with the advertising. The core competencies must improve as well.

For your business to survive in this new age of hyper-communication, you're going to have to help your marketing out by improving what you offer. You need to re-assess your product, your quality, and make great strides to become more exceptional, genuine, consistent and competitive than ever. You really have to become what they want, not what you want to sell them.

The best way to achieve this is to put a high priority on developing your brand. Today, this is your best defense against easy substitution and competitive low-pricing. You need to create the type of brand that is always known for value, quality and a great customer experience. Then, throw a little marketing on that and you'll have a great combination.

2

BRANDING

*"A brand is not what you think it is;
it's what <u>they</u> think it is."*

Branding Characteristics

Package of Belief

A brand is a mental "Package of Beliefs" we form over time about companies or products. It is used to categorize and rate each in our mind. This can be based on personal experience, things we have heard from trusted sources, through research, or even what we've been told by their advertising and marketing. In this package, we put experiences and perceptions that immediately pop into our head whenever we see or hear the company name.

How Brands Are Born

A company develops a brand as soon as it is introduced to the consumer's mind. It starts as simple as the condition of your website, how clean your bathrooms are, or how they were greeted when they entered your store. It's their perception of what to expect when dealing with any particular brand. It can even be their "gut feeling". These perceptions can develop simply through a manifestation of your actions or reputation, or what you have tried to present about yourself through advertising.

A Brand is Genuinely Earned

Whatever people think about you, you earned it. You might be able fool folks for a short while, but sooner rather than later, the truth emerges.

- If you do or don't deliver quality, it becomes part of your brand.
- If you do or don't deliver good service, that becomes part of your brand.
- If you do or don't deliver what they want or what is valued, that becomes your brand.

Your brand is not what you say you are; it's what _they_ say you are. In this world of new communication, you've become transparent and exposed. You can't hide the truth very long.

Wise companies are realizing they can no longer let their brands just wander around. Too much is now at stake. Taking control of your brand through good research, planning and quality improvement will build your company's staying power.

Differentiating Value

A brand is used by an organization to identify and distinguish its products and/or services from the competition.

Differentiation is not a new concept. It actually got its start in the 1940's in early television. Back in the 1980's Jack Trout and Steve Riven called it "The Tyranny of Choice" in their book _Differentiate or Die_.

Branding

They observed, "With nearly one million branded products in the marketplace today, consumers have more choices than they know how to handle. Companies must give customers the tools they need in purchasing decisions to draw them to their products."

The tools are *the features* your company, product or service possesses which are buyer-relevant and unique from your competition. If these don't exist, you're down to a lowest price comparison—a bidding war.

Positioning

Positioning is a term often used with differentiating value. Positioning is the process of creating a unique or elevated image or identity of your product, service, brand, or organization in the minds of your target market.. Here are some examples of brands that have positioned themselves well:

Product	Category	Brand Position	Differentiating Value
7UP	Soft Drink	The Un-Cola	Not just another soft drink
Jeep	Automobile	the 4-wheeler	Not just another SUV
Harley-Davidson	Motorcycle	the status bike	Not just another motorcycle
Special K	Cereal	the diet cereal	Not just another cereal
Budweiser	Beer	The King of Beers	Not just another beer
Campbell's Soup	Soup	MMM... Good!	Not just another soup

All these companies were able to position themselves apart from competitors in their categories and embed *one thing* you automatically attach to their name when you hear it. Your brand should strive to move you out of the "just another" status. This differentiation can often translate into sales.

Brand Equity

Brand equity is where a company, product or service has gained the advantage of common first or second recall, and/or instant recognition. In the extremely successful cases, company brands are even used as the common *description* of the product.

- Kleenex
- Heinz
- Google it
- Band-Aid
- Scotch tape

Brand equity is usually created over time or by being first and heavily promoted. This recognition translates into huge advantages to its owners. Can you even think of a brand that competes with Band-Aids?

When a company is sold, brand equity can be the most expensive component. If you were to buy Frito Lay, you could buy the factory and the equipment to duplicate the product for a fraction of what you would pay to buy the brand itself. The hard part of mass awareness and acceptance has already been done. Everyone is aware of you, knows where to find you, can mentally recall how your products taste; even how to use them within recipes.

You should aspire to build equity in your brand. In your home town, you should try to get folks to reference you as the common choice. When you need your car fixed you go to Jones Brothers. When you want pie you go to Peggy's. If you're living in Springfield, Missouri, and you want great ice cream anyone will tell you to go to Andy's. You just can't buy that kind of advertising.

Equity is built on quality, on delivering or exceeding expectations. Advertising and marketing can only reinforce it; they cannot build it for you. When you have built trust and loyalty, you build brand equity, and that builds financial stability in your company.

Branding Advantages

Brand Implies Reduces Risk

Change makes people nervous. When we find something we like, most of us tend to stay with it. Why? Because change means risk—and most of us don't like taking more risks than we have to.

When making a purchase, consumers face two primary risks:

1. Am I paying a fair price?
2. Will this perform as it's represented or as I expect it to perform?

An established and recognized brand provides a safe port for the shopper. This recognition implies less risk. A recognized brand reinforces (and even exaggerates) your company's longevity, which implies other people believe and are satisfied with your service or product.

The Mckinsey Quarterly report I mentioned earlier also stated that consumer purchases are based 60% on the company brand, and only 40% on the product itself.

A good brand will also have a very direct effect on the Return on Investment (ROI) in your advertising dollars. I call this Effective Selling Time (see below).

Branding Allows You to Charge More

With less risk comes greater value. If your product or service has a more recognizable and positive brand than competitors, people are willing to pay more.

Customers Stay Loyal To Brands

People like to stay with a winner. Therefore, you don't have to spend as much money to get repeat or referral business from your customers. Loyalty also insolates you from your competitions offers.

Customers Are More Receptive To Brand Extensions

Once you have established loyalty, buyers will also be more receptive to the introduction of new products or services from a brand they trust more than from one they don't recognize. This will substantially reduce the cost of product introduction.

Effective Selling Time

Effective Selling Time is the **measurement of time that a prospect is tuned in and receptive to an offer.** The quicker and more positively a prospect recognizes your brand, the more Effective Selling Time you'll have to pitch to them.

Every time a consumer sees an advertisement they must:
1. Process through recognizing who or what the ad is about,
2. Search their memory for information or history about who is running the ad, then
3. Decide what level of confidence they will place in the message they are receiving.

Another way to look at this is: when a prospect does not recognize your brand, they get stuck in the mud. They question who you are, whether they have heard of you, or if you are even worth considering, etc. The longer they do this, the less time they have to consider your offer. I call this Un-Effective Selling Time "The Jury Zone" (As if the jury is still out deciding your fate.)

Branding

Jury Zone

Effective Selling Time

When the prospect easily recognizes a well-branded company, they skip over this jury process, which leaves more time for them to more closely examine and consider the subject offer. What we're talking about is an element of timing—if the prospect knows your brand, they will spend all their time considering your offer.

Consider the following example for a better understanding of this concept:

 See this? In a Nano-second you recognized this as McDonalds, and the jury considered the evidence:

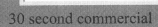
30 second commercial

JURY ZONE	EFFECTIVE SELLING TIME
•Convenient locations •Fast service •Good food •Clean restaurants •Ronald McDonald •Consistent Food	 

You didn't have to think about it long before you were ready to hear them talk about their new shamrock shakes, McRib sandwich or remind you to come in and get some of those great French fries. They're pitching and you're listening.

Now, consider this:

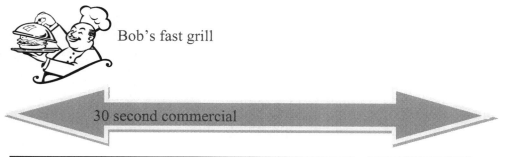

Bob's fast grill

30 second commercial

JURY ZONE
- What the heck is this?
- Who are these guys?
- Are they clean?
- Where are they?
- Are they expensive?
- I've never heard of them before.

EFFECTIVE
S E L L I N G
TIME

Bob could be superior in every aspect to McDonalds. But if his brand is not as recognizable to new prospects, Bob is going to lose the war. Look at the math.

Just like football is a game of inches; advertising is a game of seconds. The average television commercial is :30 seconds long; radio ads run between :30 and :60; an average print ad gets roughly :02.3 seconds of consideration; billboards get about :03 seconds. You don't have a lot of time to make an impression on your audience.

If you pay $100 for an ad, and 75 percent of the time your prospect is trying to figure out who you are, searching their memory banks for if

Branding

they've ever heard of you, where you're located, any past history they might have with you, and evaluating if they would do business with you (jury zone), that leaves you with only 25 percent Effective Selling Time in your ad to pitch your product. Basically, your ad was 25 percent effective. So you would have to run four ads and spend $400 dollars to get 100 percent worth of effective selling time.

Now, your competitor who has an established brand runs a similar advertisement. Immediately, the prospect recognizes your competitor (the jury goes out and come right back in), and is tuned in and ready to receive the details about their offer. Your competitor's ad was around 10 percent jury zone and 90 percent effective selling time.

Therefore, you would have to outspend your competitor by four times to get the same result with the same offer. This is why it is so difficult and expensive to try to knock an established competitor off the top of the mountain. RC Cola will never dethrone Coca-Cola—they just don't have the budget to take them on and to replace the brand image of Coca-Cola in the jury's mind.

Brand Elements

Branding elements are used to form a visual and/or audible identification of your brand. These elements are not used as a reason to buy as much as to form an immediate recognition. They can be the use of colors, graphic design, slogans, sounds, jingles, consistent spokesperson, etc.

Seeing or hearing this immediately puts recognition of something or somebody in your head. Remember your Uncle Bob who had that cool Harley-Davidson? All you had to do was hear a Harley rumble and it triggered your memory to think about Uncle Bob.

Visual branding elements can be very simple. Consider a billboard displaying nothing more than a red background with two golden arches. Unless you grew up on another planet, you immediately recall

McDonalds. It doesn't have to mention price, product, or anything other than those arches for your mind, to recognize that a McDonald's must be in the area. And now you're hungry.

An audio example may be a jingle associated with your brand or product (*"Things go better with Coke"*). The more people humming that jingle while driving to work, the better the odds you'll move up in the recall pecking order when they're getting thirsty. Creating good branding elements that improve recall boost advertising ROI.

The Marketing Department at USC produced a study showing a 33 percent improvement in recall of advertisements with jingles compared to those without jingles. Do the math. This means you can run the ad two-thirds as often and still get the same recall benefit. What would you save by reducing your broadcast advertising budget by a third?

Unique Sales Proposition (USP)

Brands contain feature/benefits that are used to support your brand value through differentiation. It's a more detailed description of the qualities that are advantageous or unique to a particular product or service (Differentiating Value) in a way that will compel customers to purchase it rather than similar rivals. When used in your promotion or advertising, they help to separate and elevate your brand above others.

Strong USP's in your brand help in many ways. A couple examples are:

- We gain easier recall in the prospect's mind.
- Branding ourselves to an advantageous USP gives us an "ownership" of that particular advantage, making it difficult for competitors to use in their advertising.

A USP creates a "perception or framed reference" of what you offer and the benefits to the buyer. That perception can give you great advantage, but remember you MUST be able to prove or demonstrate it upon the first time a customer purchases or the public will soon brand you as a liar or a cheat.

Some examples that could set you apart are:
- The provable lowest price
- The provable highest quality
- Something that makes you exclusive
- A reputation for providing superior customer service
- A provable larger selection
- Providing the best guarantees

I'll show you how you identify and formulate your USPs later in the chapter.

Ego-Centric USP'S

Do you know why most websites really don't convert many prospects to customers? I think it is because websites are horribly boring braggers. They lead off with me – me – me. *"I have this feature and that feature, I've been in business since 1901, I've got all these letters behind my name, etc."*

Advertising features without a tie-in to a benefit are generally reflected by the prospect. People won't care about your features, cool tools or extensive processes you incorporated into your products, unless they understand how those features provide a **benefit to them**.

For instance:
- ***"We're the biggest!"***—*I don't care* that your dry cleaning business has more employees than the other chains. Good for you, but what does that do for me? I won't care unless you further explain that with all this additional help, you clean my shirts in one day, and not three like smaller shops.

- ***"Employee owned!"***—*I don't care* that you are employee owned – unless you further demonstrate that produces better customer service ratings.
- ***"Winner of the Frank Miller Award for Excellence!"***—*I don't care* that your hospital won the Frank Miller Award for Excellence. Who the heck is Frank Miller? What is the award based on? How will that affect me?

While some features may be important issues which buyers may or may not consider in the process, don't force them to think about how to convert your features into benefits they value. If you do, you only produce what I call ego-centric branding or advertising. You're just pounding your chest. (On the other hand, these types of advertisements would be very useful indeed if directed internally to staff as a motivational message and/or when used as a recruitment tool! Again, the recognition of the USP as something important to the targeted audience.)

Also, if you have to go into great explanation to tie the benefit to the feature, remember we don't have a lot of patience or long attention spans. While this is prudent and necessary when promoting more technical or complex products to higher educated prospects, it's generally a bad rule for the rest of us.

The old slogan: "Sell the sizzle, not the steak" is a good rule to remember when developing your USPs. It's okay to start with the feature, but show the customer what they get out of it.

Practice What You Preach

Some companies try to create USPs from their personal beliefs or mission statements. They use their advertising to try to convince us they are unique, with lofty ideals or principles they don't actually practice. Few things are more aggravating to me than to be the sixth cart back in

Branding

the only open check-out lane in a store that has a banner saying: "Serving you is our Passion."

I recently had a similar scenario occur when I flew into LAX. On this last visit, I was one of 30 people standing in line to rent a car for over 35 minutes. There were 25 rental-counters with only five clerks waiting on people. There were five other employees talking with each other, looking at their PCs, but didn't try to pitch in and help reduce the backlog.

I was thinking to myself that most of these employees probably were trained on customer service at the DMV when I noticed a big sign on their wall. It was a survey that named this rental company as No. 1 in Customer Satisfaction, among many other quality claims. Since this is the third time in a row I've seen this lack of urgency and indifference to customers at this same rental company, I tried to YELP my opinion of that survey so fast I almost broke my thumbs. So was the lady in front of me, and the couple behind me. I didn't actually complete my online complaint because there were so many already against this company, it seemed pointless. Upon returning home, I made sure we never again used that company. This is the kind of customer experience you don't want for your business.

Live By Value or Die By Price

USP's should be used to demonstrate differentiating value in more ways than just the lowest price. If you are not, you'll find you're too often in a bidding war with rivals who may not have your overhead to support, or can undercut your prices through higher volume or lower cost to produce. Remember, today you are competing with products or services that can be produced or provided by low-labor countries or larger retailers.

While price is important, people look for many things when making a buying decision. The advertiser who can communicate to the prospects that they satisfy more of the prospects' needs than simply offering a low price will grow market share.

Unfortunately, most businesses practice "Copycat" advertising strategies. They mimic the same strategy that they've see others do, defusing any differentiation whatsoever between them. The only decision point the buyer can look to is where they can buy it cheaper. Thus, it creates the never-ending bidding war.

A prime example of copycat advertising is often found in the grocery business. The typical grocery store's sole advertising is a weekly newspaper or handout publications that only promote price and product. It's the same thing every grocery store does, every week.

However, a study from a grocery store trade publication revealed that price is not even the number one reason people pick a grocery store; *it's number two!* There are 15 other things people consider that are almost as important. The margin of preference between number 1 and number 15 is only 12 percent.

Location, convenience, service, even store layout are as important, if not more important than price to the average grocery shopper. Yet the grocery stores continue to do the same old low-price song and dance as everybody else. That's not marketing; that's a bad habit.

As a rule, grocery store managers all complain about their small margins of profit. Remember me saying something about people want more than just a low price? And that without demonstrating another value you're only creating your own bidding wars? I'm not saying you wouldn't have to continue to be very price-sensitive, but just a little bit more for all of those apples can add up and increase those tiny margins.

Does Kroger's lower price on seedless grapes make you choose them over Stop & Shop? I don't think so. The smart grocery store might want to take another look at their own research and start trying to position itself as the store that provides more of the things people want besides

Branding

price. Again, I'm not saying they can knee-jerk and withdraw from price comparison, but expand their communications to promote the other things they do that are important to their buyers.

Grocery stores are a good example of "copycat" advertising, but many other businesses, from fast food chains to healthcare providers do the same thing to more or lesser degrees.

How to Find Your USPs

Unless you have the budget to purchase research or the time and skill to conduct Focus Groups, it can be hard to identify your USPs. Often the similarities between competing businesses and services are so close that there appears to be little differentiating value provided by any of them.

If you're going to try to determine USPs without data, start by identifying the features you believe you can provide to your customers that your competition cannot, or at least what you can do better than the competition. Remember, these must be features that you can convert to benefits that would be relevant and valuable to the buyer, not just something you think is cool.

Here is a simple outline you can use to help you find and capitalize on your company's most powerful USPs.

1. List your unique or important features
   - We have reasonable prices.
   - We have a **large selection**.
   - We have a **convenient location** near a **freeway**.
   - We **guarantee** our products.
   - We have **express checkout** (10 items or less).
   - We have a **garden section**.
   - We have **easy parking**.
   - We're **open until 10:00 p.m.**

Marketing Survival in a Digital World

2. **Competitive comparison**: The next step is to identify which of these features your competition offers. When you find something the public wants that competitors don't offer or that you can clearly demonstrate you do better, you have an opportunity to create a USP for advertising promotion.

Let me show you how a home improvement store might handle this. Again, honesty and impartiality are critical here.

Our Store	Competitor A	Competitor B
We have reasonable prices.	Yes	Yes
We have large selection.	No	Yes
We have a convenient location near a free-way.	No	No
We guarantee our products.	Yes	Yes
We have express checkout (10 items or less).	Yes	Yes
We have a garden section.	No	Small
We have easy parking.	Yes	Yes
We're open until 10:00 p.m.	No	No

3. Rate the importance of your unique features (according to your buyers)

Now you've identified four unique features you have over your competitors. However, unique does not necessarily mean valuable. You now should try to rate the importance of these features to your core audience.

Remember, you're trying to identify the ***most important, relevant*** and ***appealing*** things your audience wants or needs. In essence you're

Branding

trying to find which of these features can be converted into a true marketable benefit to your consumers.

Rate the features for importance as high, medium or low.

Importance	Rating	Benefits
We have large selection.	High	• Save time • Save gas
We have a convenient location near a freeway.	High	• 60 percent of our customer base lives out of town and would use the freeway • Quicker and easier to get to
We have a garden section.	High	• Improves: • Home value • Atmosphere • Grow your own vegetables • Gives you something to do • A sense of pride
We're open until 10:00 p.m.	Medium to low	• Most people have finished shopping by that time of night

So now you've determined a value rating and benefit point for each of your four unique features.

Typically, this is as far as most business will think it through before they start promoting them. This should not be done yet. Features need to be converted to benefits! This is why you see so much advertising that looks like this:

Feature only USP
- The largest selection!
- Convenient location!
- Garden section!
- Open until 10pm!

How many times have you seen these features claimed by stores? How likely are you to remember these features? Can you tie them to any particular store that you can recall? Are these strong enough marketing positions that they can help your advertising or promotion rise above the noise of other competitors advertising? I don't think so.

It is very important to take the identified features to the next level by associating them with benefits the customers will recognize and desire!

Feature/Benefit USP

- *Save time and gas* with our huge selection!
- Convenient location gets you here quicker!
- *Beautify your home* with our garden section!
- Open until 10:00 p.m. *to fit your busy schedule!*

These are certainly a noticeable improvement over the typical "feature only" USP approach. Tying in the benefits helps the customer see immediate value to them. They will actually appreciate that you've saved them brain-work and you'll probably be rewarded with more shoppers.

Think about it. Between all the problems at work and home, the budgeting, taking care of the family, etc., don't you appreciate it when someone says, "I can help *and here is how it will benefit you!*"? People appreciate stuff that is easier on the brain and will respond positively.

Positioning Your USP with Creative

A more advanced approach to positioning your USP is adding elements of *discovery or entertainment.*

Discovery is the introduction or a twist on a benefit the consumer had not considered. Entertainment approaches the prospect in a less obvious selling-mode. It reduces the threat, relaxes the senses and opens the mind to an un-obtrusive proposal.

Branding

Both of these tactics attempt to set your feature/benefit USP on a different level within the mind. It helps to further separate and elevate your offerings from your competitors, as well as suggest and imply higher benefits and value to the consumer.

This is where good creative steps in. Let me show you by creatively positioning the previously discussed USPs.

Feature/benefit USP
- Save time and gas with our huge selection!

Creative Positioning USP
- With selection this big, bring your GPS.
- You cannot not find what you're looking for
- Yep, we've got that too!

With each of these, we've set the features and the benefits in ways that create images that demonstrate (position) the feature (USP) without saying it like everyone else. Adding the positioning image of a GPS in your store screams "biggest selection!" And thereby ties the ownership of this important feature/benefit to you more than your competitors.

Feature/benefit USP
- Convenient location gets you here quicker!

Creative Positioning USP
- Here Quicker. Fixed Quicker.

Again, this doesn't have to even mention freeway. And you've positioned the benefit that helps them "discover" they'll the get job done sooner when they shop with you. Just saying convenient freeway access would not have accomplished that, would it?

Feature/benefit USP
- Beautify your home with our garden section!

Creative Demonstration USP

- We Give Your Home Flower-Power
- Patio-Fresh Vegetables Sold Here
- Summer Never Tasted So Good
- Made In The Shade

Do you see? Instead of thinking garden section they're now thinking healthy eating, beauty, relaxing shade. Things they want, but may not have immediately associated with your offering.

Feature/benefit USP

- Open until 10:00 p.m. to fit in your busy schedule!

Demonstration USP

- Your Late-Leak Solution Store
- Say Goodbye to After-Hour Service Charges

In each example above, you've out-flanked your competition and gained an ownership of an important USP because of creative positioning of the benefits.

A couple of other advantages are:

- Competitors can't duplicate your positioning approach or they look like copycats. Playing follow the leader implies your product or service is second rate.
- Once you have positioned your USP, it is very expensive to take it away from you. People don't like change. It is often estimated it would require twice to ten times the advertising investment to demote the leader who owned the position first in the consumer's mind. So if they want to own it after you have it, it's really going to cost them.

Branding using creatively positioned USPs make your advertising more effective and increases your Effective Selling Time. Find out what your prospects want, identify which of these things you do better than the

Branding

competition, position it creatively and then shout it from the mountain until they hear you and believe you own it.

Building Your Brand

Branding begins with research. You must gain a true and clear understanding of your current situation to understand where your brand position is strong or flawed.

You should know how your prospects and customers perceive your brand—their levels of trust and utilization. Customer satisfaction surveys and/or focus groups can give you a lot of insight as to how they view your company, product or services, what they would change, and what else they need that you might deliver.

You must also understand your competitors, their brand position, market share, etc. Shopping them yourselves, using focus groups to compare, and using any published reports that give an indication of sales volumes, all help you formulate a better picture of what you're up against. Don't take your competition for granted.

Based on the above, you must discuss and decide your direction and your brand objectives. You're basically trying to guide your reputation by determining "How do I want to be perceived, and what do I have to accomplish to do this?" You must honestly determine if what you decide is a good fit for your company and your employees, and if it is achievable. You need to identify what would stand in your way, what you have to correct, and then develop a plan and processes outlining how to get there. You must make certain that what you promise through your brand is delivered operationally, or all your marketing work will have little to no impact in the end. Remember, you must be genuine to what you say.

As you develop communication concepts for your new brand, share these with a select few decision makers before you reveal it to everyone. Design should be strategic, but still is highly subjective. Let a few make a decision and avoid logo-by-committee. Trying to design around too many opinions can produce a very confused message.

You should reveal and promote your brand internally, before you send it to the target audience. You must gain buy-in from employees or your brand will not take hold. They need to agree and implement process/behavior modifications to deliver on the brand promise.

Once your brand takes hold internally, you can reveal it to the target audience. A good marketing plan should outline campaigns, messages, media, timing and budgets. You should also have pre-determined measurement thresholds for online to continually measure your new brand's effectiveness. Adjust as necessary, but don't stray from your brand position.

3

RESEARCH

"Measure twice, cut once." – Sam Walton

Marketing is as much about research and planning as it is about communication. Marketing research provides the critical reality-check to help decision makers understand both their current situation and the true challenges and potential ahead.

Too often business owners and managers create great aspirations and expectations about their future, their market position, or what services they will provide or products they will sell without sufficient evidence (research) that it is even achievable. When they call upon their advertising to "communicate" and to generate sales, it fails or has no measurable impact.

Then the "Blame Game" begins. Smaller entrepreneurs blame their media. Mid-sized to larger companies blame their marketing departments or advertising agency.

Why? What happened? Where did communications miss the mark?

Maybe it didn't. Simply the omission of proper research can doom even the best advertising communications.

- What if there was no or very limited demand? Can communication alone create and sustain a market? Can you sell ice to an Eskimo?
- What if your quality or service is bad or you can't deliver what you promise? Can good communication keep dissatisfied buyers returning?
- What if consumers have found your competitor better at providing the same thing you offer? Can communication continually convince people to go against their better judgment?

Quantitative Reports

Quantitative research uses data and general results from a sample of the target population or prospects. It shows common and frequent *patterns of views and opinions*. It normally includes results from a large number of cases of randomly selected respondents. Statistical data is usually in the form of tabulations (tabs). Findings are conclusive and usually descriptive in nature and most often used to recommend a final course of action. Qualitative research often follows to explore some *reasons for* views and opinions.

The data can be gathered yourself through on-street or telephone interviews, or using online survey software such as Survey Monkey (http://www.surveymonkey.com/) or Snap Surveys (http://www.snapsurveys.com/). The information can also be supplied by a research vendor such as National Research Corporation (https://hcmg.nationalresearch.com/Default.aspx) or NRC Information Online (http://nrc.hu/eng).

Research

Surveys

When conducting a survey, you need to ensure:

- You're asking the right questions that will enable you to arrive at clear conclusions. There is a real art to the phrasing of the questions and the number you ask.
- You're not "leading" the answers to what you want to hear. You've got to stay unbiased if you intend to really learn anything. If you need affirmation, call your mother.
- You've got the time to actually conduct it and compile it. When comparing the cost of conducting an in-house survey to that of a professional firm, in the end you might be surprised you didn't save much money. A good survey is not simple and does not run itself. You're going to have to do it yourself (which produces opportunity loss) or hire an employee or vendor.
- You use a large enough sample. There is no set number. You're going to have to determine how much is enough. If you need a recommended guess, I'd say no less than 40 complete responses per survey.
- You have a quality sample. The responders should be qualified to be selected responders. You wouldn't simply pick names out of the yellow pages to conduct a survey for preferences regarding chemical hazard disposal options (if the results are to be truly meaningful).

Qualitative Research

Qualitative research usually follows quantitative research to gain an understanding of underlying reasons and motivations often based on the quantitative results. The research is often obtained from conducting a Focus Group.

Focus Groups

Conducting focus groups is another method you can use to gain insight on people's attitudes or perceptions. Commonly used for new product development, focus groups typically have 8 to 12 people and are controlled by one moderator.

There are many variations from mini-groups to dueling moderators. Here are basic steps to conducting a standard focus group, which is most commonly used.

1. The first step is to develop a questionnaire for the session. You might also want to provide additional material to be used during the sessions.
2. The next step is to decide on how many people you need in your sample? If you need 12 or more, you should consider conducting multiple sessions. You don't want them larger because you won't get equal participation as the size increases.
3. You must also qualify the people that you invite, so you're certain to get the opinions of those audiences that are relevant to the subject matter.
4. You need to select an unbiased moderator who can control the sessions and extract answers. **The moderator is probably the most important element of this effort.**
5. Select a location that is convenient and appropriate.
6. Set up recording devices, but keep them out of sight. You may not always get frank and honest answers if the audience is intimidated about being recorded.
7. You need to find a method of targeting and contacting your participants. This could be done by telephone calls, through the mail or online to groups where you have email addresses. This will also require a follow-up to confirm attendance just prior to the sessions.

8. You may also need to provide some incentive to the participants. Currently, $50 seems to be the magic number for general population survey sessions. However, you're not going to get many attorneys, physicians or architects to participate with that amount.

Market Demand

Quite often I've seen many start-up businesses that are doomed to fail before they open their doors. They base their existence (and have probably bet their 401ks) on selling a product that either has very limited demand, or is really more of a passing fad.

Back in the 1960's a shrewd marketer put a rock in a box and called it a pet rock. Inside there was a slip of paper certifying you were adopting this rock and would give it a good home (or something like that). This is a great example of the fact you *can* create market demand as a *fad*, but you cannot sustain it. The rock made it's originator a million bucks, but was off the shelves in a year. There simply was no demand beyond the original hype, so continuing to advertise and market this fad after the buzz wore off would have been a waste of money.

The most ironic thing is many entrepreneurs have it in their heads that just because they start or go into business *that there is sustainable demand*. Opening your doors does not create demand. You need to conduct brutally-honest research to determine true demand, competition, economic conditions, etc. Before you open or invest a dime in promotion.

I realize this may sound contradictory to earlier statements such as "give them what they want" or even "be ready to change." The key difference regarding change is you start with a core that has *sustainable demand*, then making changes that are extensions of the core product or service; not one-shot wonders.

Even if your product does have long-life potential or longevity, you must also ensure there is *sufficient demand* whereby you can earn enough to pay yourself and the overhead. This is not just predicated on the product or service, but the degree of competition you face.

You could also have an established business that produces goods and services that simply aren't wanted anymore. You have either not recognized the true decline in market demand, or you saw it coming but didn't have a good plan to reinvent yourself in time.

Fortunately, online gives marketers the same researching advantage that consumer's use, along with a growing selection of sophisticated research options. It provides new ways to conduct surveys and engage directly with buyers to ask questions.

You can easily locate relevant opinions and discussion in blogs, on Facebook pages, online groups, etc. You can also locate specific studies, or find research companies that can do them for you.

One very useful research tool is using Google AdWords. This feature will tell you how many keyword searches are being conducted for different keywords or key phrases, right down to a specific area. For instance, you may want to know how many monthly searches are conducted for snow tires nationwide or in your town. From this you will be able to have a better indication of demand based on the number of folks searching within a 30-day period.

Another useful way to conduct research is Google Analytics, a free tool you can (and really should) install on your website. It reports how much traffic your site gets, how many pages people view, how long they stay, etc. While this does not give you a good indication of demand within a geographic area, it is useful in that it delivers very good indications of how your website it performing, and/or measure peoples interest levels in your products.

Here's just one example how Google Analytic data can change a marketing strategy:

Research

I had a client who owned a motorcycle dealership. He spent a significant amount of money every month on advertising his new lines like Yamaha and Honda, but didn't ever mention his used inventory. In January of 2009, the economy hit the skids. People were worried about keeping jobs, and didn't have as much disposable income. New bike sales came to a screeching halt seemingly overnight.

We worked on the client's website and installed Google Analytics. This gave us the ability to measure visitor activity and a good indication of their preferences.

What immediately jumped out was that almost twice as many people who visited his website were viewing his used inventory over his new inventory. It seems that more people were looking for used because they thought it would be more affordable and easier to make payments.

So I suggested featuring his used line in his ads instead of the new product nobody was looking for (duh). A couple of months later, most automotive dealers in the country moved their advertising dollars to feature their used cars because that is what was selling.

By simply monitoring visitor behavior on his website, we found a large market demand was not being addressed, and we did it before his competitors did. Often that can be the difference between survival and folding.

Research is ongoing. It never ends as long as you're in business.

Competitive Research

Most of your competitors don't like you. I mean, they'll smile and shake your hand at the Chamber of Commerce mixers, but they really prefer you weren't around. And they are going to try to outsell you at every turn.

In business, you've got to be a bit tough to handle tough competition. You must learn as much as you can about the companies trying to take your clients or customers. Competitive research will also tell you many important things about yourself. You'll start to see patterns about how you measure up against the rest. It will help you make better decisions on improving your own quality, or the products or services you offer.

Most importantly, you'll also find niches of opportunities; unfulfilled needs that if moved on quickly, could position you in profitable situations even in a competitive marketplace.

Many years ago, I became vice president of marketing for a residential building and development firm. We were in a market that was one of the fastest growing in the United States. At its peak, there were over 90 subdivisions marketing in the same area at the same time. And all the heavyweights were there; Brock, Kaufmann & Broad, US homes, Pardee, etc. The company I worked for didn't have nearly the marketing budget those giants enjoyed. I couldn't outspend them, so I concluded we had to out-think them.

First, I researched the heck out of my competitors. I visited every subdivision, walked through every model home; I even secretly videotaped them. I took all this data and scrutinized it; looking for every advantage, every unfulfilled need or niche.

Using this information, we were able to create a product line that was unique in this highly-competitive market. We carried the theme into our model traps and sales offices to create a more unique and entertaining shopping experience than others offered.

In the end, we outsold the competition 2:1. When I released a new phase, I actually had to have college football players guarding the doors to keep the buyers in line. Life was good.

All of this was not based on brilliant creative. It was primarily the research which revealed the opportunities. We found un-fulfilled demand, threw some creative presentation on it, and delivered it to customers. They ate it up.

Research

These days, you can save yourself a lot of travel and gasoline by conducting much of the research online. The Internet has made research so much easier and accurate than ever before. Work to become an excellent browser!

- Look at their websites, their YouTube videos, their blogs, etc. What do they offer? Is their product better, faster, less expensive? Look at similar websites outside of your area, particularly in larger cities (where the competition normally requires exceptional marketing). Get ideas before they hit your hometown.
- Where do your competitors appear in the search engines? What keywords do they use to position themselves? Do they use Pay Per Click (PPC), retargeting, banners, webinars? Can you subscribe to their email or direct marketing list? Sign up and see what they're doing.
- Check out their online reputation and reviews. What does the public think of them or their products? Are there comparative reviews available?
- How do they market themselves? How do they position themselves? What is the essence of their brand? Trust? Quality? Price?
- What do your competitors do best? In what areas are they weak? Are there niche areas you could use to your advantage?

Once again, if you'll take the time to research and investigate your competition and market *before you spend any money*, you'll have greater success in planning your offerings and advertising campaigns.

Customer Profiling

"Aim small, miss small" – Mel Gibson in "The Patriot"

Profiling is fair in marketing. Men, women, black, white, gay, straight, rich, poor, religious, atheist, or people who are striped like a zebra, you must aim at the proper targets. It is not a judgment or a discriminating act. It is a focus on what already exists. And the closer in you can focus, the better the results.

Any given product or service does not appeal or apply to everybody equally. So why advertise to those people who will never use your product or service? That would be a waste of advertising money, right? Yet, many businesses do it all the time.

One of the most costly and overlooked planning stages is determining *who you should be targeting* as customers. Too often, business owners either guess at who their market includes or don't consider the question at all. They advertise to anyone and everyone, employing a "shotgun blast" approach to advertising that generates a great deal of expense with little return. Advertising to "everybody" is very, very expensive.

The trick to successful marketing is to isolate your most profitable or best potential slice of the "everybody pie," and focus your advertising dollars on them. Start with the low-lying fruit. Gaining market share in these groups—whether they are defined by demographics, psychographics or geographical boundaries—will increase the odds of your advertising success and increase your ROI. Often, you will still gain exposure to secondary target segments, *but you should always focus advertising dollars on targeting the bigger returns first.*

To reach qualified prospects with your advertising, you must have a clear idea of who they are. This will help you select the right media, create the right message, and ultimately improve your closing ratio.

Sometimes your target audience will be very "tight," or a specific segment of the public. You may be trying to reach only nurses, or men who like to hunt deer, or retirees needing electric wheelchairs. These simple characteristics make our target easier to reach with advertising and the message more directly relevant to them. Most of these groups have specialized magazines, publications, or websites just for them. Some targets even have specific cable shows or channels they like to watch. It just takes a little research and knowledge about your customer to find them. You have to know where your audience is looking for your product before you can advertise it to them.

Many larger businesses need to take into account multiple and separate demographics, and advertise to them differently. Take, for instance, Sears. They have items for just about everybody. Although they spend a lot of money in image advertising, the majority of the image campaigns are targeted to segments. They utilize different media and different messages to target specific buyer segments within their wide and diverse audience. Sears will send a direct mail flyer to a database of men that might buy Craftsman tools. At the same time, they may have a fall fashion clearance advertisement running nationally on television shows with a large number of female viewers. Here you have the same store trying to reach two different audiences, using different media outlets, with different creative approach in the ads.

In defining our target we need to look at three categories: demographics, geographic and psychographics.

Demographics

This covers quantifiable data about your prospects.

- Age (try to group by no more than 10 years)
- Gender
- Income
- Education
- Home ownership
- Marital status

By examining this information, you start to identify the characteristics that best fit your target prospect.

Sometimes you're not always looking for the person who makes the purchase. Often times you also need to determine who the primary influencer is.

If you run a medical clinic, all ages and gender could be your customers. However, studies show that women make medical decisions 70 percent of the time, regardless of who in the family is afflicted. Knowing this, would you want to try to use your advertising dollars to reach men and children? Probably not. In this case your dollars are best directed toward reaching more of the primary influencer – women.

Taking it a step further: knowing women with families would be more profitable prospects than single women, you probably want to focus more on women with families, right?

What about advertising auto parts? Women drive cars, but men do most of the repairs or make the decision about who is going to perform the repair. You can further segment this group to younger men, because most of them don't have the disposable income to buy newer cars like older men with more disposable income.

What about senior care? You actually have two age demographics; the seniors themselves and their children who are more likely to make care decisions on their behalf. In this instance, you're more likely to be successful targeting the decision maker (adult child) than the actual consumer of the service or product.

Sometimes in business-to-business marketing and advertising, you have to consider the position of the person you're trying to reach. Your target prospect might not be the CEO as much as the HR director, or the purchasing manager or even a department supervisor.

Research

Psychographics

Psychographic profiling is the study and classification of people according to their attitudes, aspirations, values and interests, and also includes the examination of lifestyle.

The more you understand the psychographics of your target, the more effectively you can develop the right message to influence and compel your target to purchase your product or service.

Psychographics are highly important in selecting the right media to reach your target audience and to help reduce wasted advertising dollars.

Remember, you're trying to build a profile of your prospect. Discovering more about their activities, interests and/or opinions will give you an edge. It will help you build a bridge between the company and the prospect. Here are things you may consider:

- Affiliations with clubs or groups
- Recreational interests
- Music or entertainment preferences
- Types of books or publications they would read
- Member of a particular ethnic group
- Political and/or religious preference
- Conservative or casual
- Spender or saver
- How do they typically view your product or service?

Geographic DMA

Even though online has reduced or eliminated location consideration, most small business will still have a geographical area that they consider to be their primary market. This is referred to as your designated market area (DMA). Your DMA can be within a few blocks, a city, an entire state, region, country or even international. If your business has several locations, you could have several DMAs. However, if your business is internet-based, a DMA may not apply.

While it's nice to get business from wherever you can, identifying your primary DMA helps you determine where you need to spend the bulk of your advertising budget. If your primary DMA is Philadelphia, you wouldn't want to waste money advertising in Baltimore, but you might want to include Allentown or even southern New Jersey.

You must be honest with yourself. Unless you offer a rare and highly specialized service or product, no amount of advertising is going to encourage people to drive past six competitors, from four counties away unless you're giving it away for free. Understanding your DMA is critically important when you are ready to select your advertising media. It doesn't matter that a publication has 300,000 readers if the bulk of them will never seek you out because you are 50 miles away from them and there are several more-convenient competitors.

A Simple Target Profile Example

The combined result of the demographic, geographic and psychographic data is what we normally call your target audience or profile.

Here is an example of how a target profile might be created for a hardware store.

Bob's hardware store – best customer profile

1. Demographics

Male 80%, female 20%

Men need more pictures, less copy with more bullet points. Creative for ads needs to be simple and image-heavy.

Age range: 24-55

In this example, you are dealing with men in their prime. No need for senior discounts, or approaches that may be too ado-

Research

lescent. Think more along the lines of tough, competitive, lasting, etc.

Household income: $20,000 to $40,000

Knowing this explains that price is important. They don't have a lot of disposable income, and promotion of discretionary items wouldn't be profitable. Advertise "needs," not "wants."

Education: high school with some college

Lower education requires less technical explanation, and more use of graphics and immediate gratification. "This new automatic hammer will save you time, keep your knuckles from getting bruised, and help you be more efficient."

Home owners: 40%

Your ads must be directed almost equally toward their contracting needs and personal home maintenance. Most will be in a fixer-upper. Prime example from Home Depot: "you can do it...we can help."

2. **Psychographics**

Most of our targets are blue collar, do-it-yourself types. Low price is most important, with selection and availability a close second. They don't want to read a lot, but many need advice and guidance.

They do spend a large amount of time driving, usually commuting to work. Country music is their first choice, with classic rock and heavy metal as second and third choices. Not much interest in talk radio.

Most will not subscribe to the newspaper, but will read the thrifty magazines. They like sports such as NASCAR, football, baseball and basketball. Many like hunting and fishing.

Watching network or basic cable television would be their primary relaxation time.

The demographics explained many things addressed here, but you can see their preferences help to select the best media options, as well as which product to offer and the creative format in which to offer it.

3. Geographic

Ninety percent of our clients live within 30 miles of our location.

This knowledge will help your media buying strategy. Many businesses overspend buying media that delivers a huge audience, but often well out of the service reach of the business.

Once you've created your best target profile, do a second and third, if possible. Refer to your profiles often as you make the rest of your advertising and marketing decisions to prevent wastefully spending ad dollars.

You have to understand who your prospect is, where they live, what they like, and what their values are. Once you know who you are advertising to, you can better select your media channels to reach them.

Moving Targets

Our audience, those potential customers or clients we are trying to reach, often present a moving target. All of their needs, opinions, and perceptions are constantly undergoing change. What do teenage girls wear today that they we're wearing say, five years ago? If you were going to buy a brand new car, would you expect to find cars that look like the one you drove eight years ago? Do you read the same books or watch exactly the same television shows you did three years ago?

Research

To stay on top of your game, you need to stay aware of changes in public or segment opinion and perception. It is often difficult to keep your eye on them, or predict where their preferences are headed. Sometimes they can change right under your nose.

4

ADVERTISING

I believe it's important to reiterate that advertising is not dead. It is still an effective marketing communication. The point I was trying to make earlier in the section called "The Decline of Advertising" is that you can no longer lean on it like a crutch. It will not carry a company as it used to before Fragmentation and Online entered the game.

Although advertising is risky, working in conjunction with a good brand and good online components, it is still a good choice to attract and promote interest in a product or service.

Remember this: When you buy advertising, you're buying audience.

1. You want the audience to be the closest match to your target market
2. Use the media that can deliver your message in the manner required
3. Buy that audience as cheaply as you can

You must also remember two other critical rules:

1. Use exceptional creative in the message
2. Run the ads frequently

Marketing Survival in a Digital World

A few years ago, a team from the Wharton School of Business at the University of Pennsylvania in Philadelphia set out to establish some definitive answers regarding advertisers. Several companies, including Pepsi, Frito-Lay, Colgate-Palmolive and a host of others, collectively invested more than $1 million so that Wharton might track the ROI experienced by several dozen small businesses as a result of advertising. These businesses were scientifically monitored and measured for seven years. The final report filled more than 2,500 pages. The report reached only three conclusions:

1. **There is no direct correlation between dollars invested and results gained.** In other words, how much you spend and your expected returns are not directly linked by any kind of mathematical equation. (This conclusion was different than that of USC Marshall School of Business. Either way, it's extremely minor if it exists at all.)

2. **Results are inextricably linked to the message.** Two advertisers invest the same amount of money reaching the same target audience. One succeeds brilliantly and buys the mansion on the hilltop. The other fails miserably, receiving no response whatsoever. The difference between the two was in the message of their ads.

   Ads that speak to the heart of the customer and touch a nerve are the ones that turn little companies into big companies. However, few people know how to write such an advertisement. Most business owners approach advertising with the goal of merely getting their name out. There is no evidence to suggest this will help you in the slightest.

   1.The Wharton study indicates that everything hinges on *the message you attach to your name*. Is your message predictable, and consequently boring? Is it believable? Is it relevant to the perceived need of the reader/listener/viewer? Tempt a dog with a

Advertising

bowl of rice, and he'll ignore you. Put a steak in the bowl, and you'll have his undivided attention. Your prospective customers are no different. What have you been putting in their bowls?

3. **Results increase with repetition.** When you've identified a message that generates a positive response and you deliver that message consistently, business growth in year two will be approximately twice the growth of year one. Growth in year three will be approximately triple the growth of year one, with growth measured in dollars, not percentages.

   But following year three, anything can happen. Your business can explode exponentially, or it can flatten out as though hitting an invisible glass ceiling. I've seen clients grow to 70 times their original size, and I've seen clients slowly grow to only double or triple their original volume and then flatten out. The difference is in the client's commitment to research and change with the changing needs of their clients, not in the ads themselves.

Advertising Budget

Budgeting is a tricky thing, especially in marketing and advertising. Too often we assume it fits neatly into a fixed percentage of sales. More often it does not. It needs to be based on the problem.

Remember the study from the Wharton School of Business stated, "There is no direct correlation between dollars invested and results gained." Results are more predicated on the message and the frequency; this easily demonstrates there is no one-size-fits-all figure.

The Fixed Percent Budget

If I ask 10 business owners or managers why they want to advertise, 9 out of 10 will simply say, *"To increase sales!"* That's a pretty good objective, but where exactly do you start?

Marketing Survival in a Digital World

Normally, they will start with a fixed budget. If I ask them what their marketing budget is, they'll throw a 3% to 5% of gross sales figure at me, or a set dollar amount that normally represent some basis of what they did last year.

This is not planning; it is simply capping a line item expense. Yet, this is basically how most small to mid-sized businesses start when formulating their marketing plans and advertising campaigns. This is bass-ackwards.

My first question is, why 3% or 5%? How do you know if this too much or too little? How will you allocate it? What media, what message, and what marketing collateral would be best for you to use? When do you apply it? Is it the same budget for a start-up as an established business?

When a new client tells me their marketing budget must fit a fixed percentage or amount, the only thing I gain is what they assume they have to work with. It does not mean it is sufficient to do the job they need. I relate it to walking into the doctor and saying, "Doc, I think I'm dying. And I have a budget of $1,000.00 to fix me."

I have seen businesses dedicate up to 50% of their sales to marketing or advertising over a limited time (such as 90 days). Their objective was to mass saturate the market with their message and capture market share. Some then ratcheted the amount of monthly investment down to around 10-25% of their gross sales for another 3-6 months.

In the cases I observed, they were very successful. They smothered their competitors with advertising Frequency and put them on the ropes. The only ones I've seen fail are those who couldn't live up to the quality or service they were advertising (and market changes for demand of course).

I'm not recommending you dedicate 50 percent of sales to marketing and advertising. I'm not recommending you start with a percentage at all.

Advertising

I recommend you focus on good Reach and Frequency with exceptional messages and offers.

Advertising Is Legalized Gambling

I believe advertising is not an exact science; it's more like legalized gambling. As such, there are no guarantees. You can roll the dice and lose everything, or gain a lot often in a short period of time. It's really no different than the same risk you take opening a business, or investing in the stock market. These too, in my opinion, are other forms of legalized gambling.

Gambling means risk. Fortunately, in many endeavors that involve risk there are still precautions or preparations you can undertake to reduce the risks. It's usually smart to begin with serious research of the subject. Then proceed with some cautious testing, measuring and adjusting as you go. Always remain keenly alert of opportunities and dangers.

The same principle applies to advertising. It is not a "set it up and run forever" proposition. It is a bottomless test tube. Applying good Frequency and great messages with great relevant offers won't eliminate your risk, but it certainly will reduce it. These principles will simply put the *odds of survival in your favor*.

You should set your budgets by a prioritized base of ***what you need to accomplish—not a fixed percent***. Once you determine and prioritize what you need to do, and then what you can actually or prudently afford to do, you'll arrive at your annual percent of sales budget.

When looking at marketing budgets, here are two rules you shouldn't forget:

1. **There is no one-size-fits-all marketing budget.**

   You've been told most businesses allocate 3-5% of sales to marketing and advertising. This is true.

According to the Small Business Association (SBA), it is also true that more than 50% of those businesses shut their doors within five years. Is this the pattern you want to follow?

In fact, these days I think it will cost most businesses a higher percentage than it did in the past. Here is my theory:

- Online has brought more competition. This increases the need to increase visibility.
- Not everything in marketing is online. Although many businesses have reduced traditional media expense, most can't completely abandon it. Competitors pick it up and fill the void. So, they have to continue traditional media usage as well as invest more online. Overall, it adds up to a higher percentage of sales.

2. **It's going to take much longer and cost more than you think to gain customers.**

Every business has different levels of consumer demand, competitors and other factors that dictate the cash you'll need to gain market share.

There is no perfect percentage or roadmap. Finding the amount truly needed is rarely done without trial and error over a sufficient time. Your goal should not be an immediate success, but rather to survive long enough to figure out how to be a long-term success.

Another option is to get some advice from a reputable and professional marketing firm. The money you'll pay for consulting up front may save you thousands in waste, or indeed save your business altogether.

Forecasting

"Most startups run out of money before they can fill up on required experience."

Advertising

Remember recent SBA studies indicate 50 percent of businesses close within five years after opening? The primary reason a business fails is poor cash flow.

Running out of cash can occur for many reasons. It could be caused by *underestimating expenses*. From my observations, I think most of the time the reason a company runs out of cash is *overstating income*.

Estimating Expense Is Easy

With prior experience, you bring in an understanding of overhead, rent, transportation costs, insurance, cost of goods and labor, taxes, etc., all of which are fairly easy to quantify and project. With some good management and bookkeeping, you can probably get your new venture off the ground and maybe turn a profit in short order (provided you have the customers).

With this prior experience, they learn a little or a lot regarding overhead, rent, transportation costs, insurance, cost of goods and labor, taxes, etc., all of which are fairly easy to quantify and project. With some good management and bookkeeping, you can probably get your new venture off the ground and maybe turn a profit in short order—provided you have the customers.

Projecting Sales Is Difficult

Projecting and acquiring customers is far less quantifiable than the operational aspects of opening a business. You can do the math and work out your break-even analysis to see exactly how many buyers you'll need each month, but what guarantee do you have that you'll get them? Exactly what can you do to ensure you'll actually get the number you project you'll need?

Naturally, you start with some good training and advice. In most cases you'll start with research like a break-even analysis, good competitive analysis, a PEST (Political, Economic, Social, and Technology) analysis, a buyer demographic, psychographic, geographic analysis, a Four P's (Product, Price, Positioning and Promotion) analysis, just to name a few. All of these steps are certainly important and prudent.

Even with this, it is very hard to accurately predict sales. You are trying to forecast human behavior in a rapidly changing competitive environment. The best you can do is continually research, measure, and test market. You must repeat this cycle for as long as you stay in business. Remember, nothing today remains static for long.

In the end, when you can't accurately predict your cash flow, you'll make bad decisions. You'll expand when you should be saving. Or you may be too conservative and miss new opportunities as they become available. Cash predictability is important.

Prospect Value Calculation Sheet

Time after time, I've seen advertising improve traffic flow for businesses who fail to convert the prospects into customers because of poor service, bad pricing, poor inventory, a dirty store, and a variety of other reasons. Typically, the marketing gets blamed and the true causes are never corrected. For this reason advertising's effectiveness should actually be measured by the **Number of Prospects** it delivers, *not the sales volumes*.

I have occasionally used the following worksheet to calculate a crude feasibility projection of the advertising expense. It tries to determine the **Value of a Prospect.**

Yes, it's crude and a bit primitive. However, it's not a bad quick calculation to get you started down the road.

Advertising

Avg. $ Customer Spends Per Visit	$75.00	
- Cost of Good Sold	$33.00	
Value of Customer First Visit	**$42.00**	**$42.00**
Amount Spent Per Return Visit	$75.00	
- Cost of Good Sold	$33.00	
Value Per Return Visit	**$42.00**	
Avg. # Return Visits Annually	3	
Annual Value of Return Visits		**$126.00**
ANNUAL CUSTOMER VALUE		**$168.00**
Customer Referrals	10%	
Cust.Referrals X Annual Customer Value	$16.80	
TOTAL REFERRAL VALUE		**$16.80**
TOTAL CUSTOMER VALUE		**$184.80**
Closing % Per Prospect	25%	
VALUE PER PROSPECT		**$46.20**
Proposed Monthly Advertising Investment	**$2,500**	
Increase in Prospects Per Month to Break Even	54	

1. **Avg. $ Customer Spends per Visit**—Determine how much a customer's first visit is worth by subtracting the cost of goods and direct expense from the average gross sale. This will yield the **Value of Customer First Visit.**

   In the example shown, the average new customer spends $75.00 on the first visit. The cost and direct expense is $33.00. So, the **Value of Customer First Visit** is $42.00.

2. **Amount Spent Per Customer Visit**—If you bring a new customer in and they like the experience, they may come back again within the

year without further advertising or marketing expense to you unless the nature of your product service prohibits it,

In the example, an average returning customer will still spend $75.00 upon each visit. The cost and direct expense is still $33.00. So, the **Value per Return Visit** is again $42.00.

Now, we estimate that the average first time customer's **Avg. # Return Visits Annually** will be three times per year. Multiplying the **Avg. # Return Visits Annually** by the **Value per Return Visit** will give you the **Annual Value of Return Visits.**

3. Combining the **Value of Customer First Visit** with the **annual value of return visits** will show you the **Annual Customer Value.** This is the gross income (minus cost and direct expense) that you can expect from every new customer in the first year of doing business with them.

4. **Customer Referrals**—Many satisfied customers will refer other people. To be fair, you need to estimate a conservative income value of referrals brought to you by a customer you gained from your advertising.

   We estimated that 1 out of 10 customers would refer somebody (i.e. 10 percent). Multiply the **Annual Customer Value** by percentage of customer referrals and you'll get a dollar figure that represents the **Total Referral Value**.

5. Adding the **Annual Customer Value** to the **Total Referral Value** shows the **Total Customer Value.** This is simply the annual value of every new customer you gain from your advertising. But we're not done.

6. **Closing % Per Prospect -** you don't close every prospect that comes through the door. Assign a number that represents your average **Closing % Per Prospect.** Then simply multiply your **Total Customer**

Advertising

Value by your **Closing % Per Prospect** to arrive at the **Value per Prospect.**

We've estimated your closing ratio is 25%. So using the 25% x **Total Customer Value** of $184.80 yields a **Value Per Prospect** of $46.20.

7. Now, you can see that if you spend $2,500 per month in advertising, you need at least 54 more prospects to break even. This translates to about two per day. Remember, this is to break-even.

The big question to ask now is "Is this feasible?" If not, why? There are many (but not too many) variables that can significantly affect the outcome. To see for yourself, set this same scenario up in an excel spreadsheet and then adjust the variables such as the cost per visit or your closing ratio. You'll see things you may have to do or improve internally before you can expect to make a return from your advertising expense.

The bottom line: You might need more customers, but you first need to determine their value before you determine your advertising budget. If each customer has a value of $200, but will not yield repeat business, you are going to have to advertise to a much broader audience to constantly bring in new customers.

Traditional Media

Prior to the explosion of the World Wide Web, newspapers, network televisions, billboards, radio and magazines were the only options we had to reach the masses. We used to refer to these as mass media. This advertising was/is used to create product awareness and generate interest to large groups of people, usually over a specific geographic area.

With the introduction of online and digital's massive reach, the term traditional media has been adopted to refer to the older advertising applications.

Advantages & Disadvantages

Traditional media has advantages and limitations. Here are a few:
General advantages:

- Reaches a large and diverse audience (wide awareness)
- Often provides opportunity for frequent exposure to audiences

General disadvantages:

- Although you may reach your target audience, you will also likely waste a large degree of your investment reaching people who are not or will not be your customers.
- With large audience reach comes more expense. Traditional media is more expensive compared to other highly-targeted marketing channels.
- The wider the audience, the less specific the message. Less specific messages often reduce compelling aspects to specific buying audiences.
- Casting a big net makes it more difficult to measure results and determine advertising ROI.
- Due to the limitations of time (:30 or :60 seconds on broadcast) or expensive print space, it typically doesn't present detailed explanations for significant evaluation.

Here are just a few comparisons by media:

Network Television

Advantages

- Television provides more credibility to the advertiser than any other media.
- It hits more of the senses—sight, sound and motion.
- Televisions are in 98.9 percent of every home in America.
- We watch an average of six hours of television per day.

Advertising

- You can target your media buy to match the shows your target audience views most often.

Disadvantages

- Commercial production is the most expensive production cost in media and takes longer to produce.

Cable television

Advantages

- Provides the same advantage as network, but the cost to buy the spots is far less than network.
- You have far more cable channels that are each targeted to different demographics. (Networks are generally targeted to everyone. The shows they run are targeted to wider demographics.)

Disadvantages

- You have less individual placement choices on the cable channels. They most often group them or sell several within price packages.
- Many homes are starting to "un-plug" from cable in lieu of online viewing through Hulu, Netflix, etc.

Radio

Advantages

- Like cable network channels, radio stations are divided by particular audience segments.
- Ability to capture audiences during drive-time
- Low-cost production, usually free with media placement buy

Disadvantages

- Listening audience is declining, particularly in younger demos. More are listening to subscription radio online or music stored on mobile devices.

Magazines and Newspapers

Advantages
- Magazines have specific reader demographics, i.e., camping, senior, guns, classic auto
- Newspapers tend to have a loyal following with older audiences

Disadvantages
- Circulation levels have declined dramatically since 2000 and will continue due to online competition. Everyday more go out of business; expect more to follow.

Billboards

Advantages
- One of the lowest cost-per-impression media.
- Good for recall and directional applications
- The ability to place in particular geographic locations

Disadvantages
- Long-term commitments
- Inability to provide more than impression value (can't educate)
- Higher production cost than most other media

Yellow Pages

Most yellow page books are dying. They are being replaced by online search engines. When was the last time you grabbed a phone book to look for a number or find a business? Anyone? Yeah, I can't remember either.

Most businesses can't rely on the phone book to drive business anymore. Take a look at the physical size of your last phone book—there are not only fewer pages and categories, but page size has shrunk to less than 8" x 11".

Advertising

The only audience who still primarily uses yellow page directories is seniors. It is an old habit that is familiar and comfortable. If your business deals with that demographic, you still may need to maintain a presence in a phone book.

Businesses that tend to provide more emergency-type situations such as plumbers, HVAC, locksmiths, etc. should also continue to maintain a small presence.

For the rest, I'm not saying pull out of the book right away, but it most cases, you should look at reducing the size of your ad and the number of books you are currently in over the next few years.

Direct Marketing

Direct marketing is another option to create awareness and interest. Although it is a form of advertising, direct marketing enables you to reach out to a specific audience rather than using a medium that reaches large groups of people.

Advantages & Disadvantages

Advantages

- Less waste—you are only paying to reach people that are likely to buy your product or service.
- More effective—your message or offer is tailored to a small group with many similarities, so it is more relevant to the prospect and therefore more effective.
- More measurable—with direct marketing you normally have better data on exactly how many prospects will be exposed to your advertising versus mass media.

Disadvantages

- Requires a database or list of recipients

Email

The number one champion of ROI in marketing and advertising is email. New contenders such as text messaging and social marketing all want a shot at the title, but (at the time of this writing) none come close to the acceptance and reach of email.

Advantages:

- Inexpensive to design
- Easy to send
- Easy to measure results
- Can contain an immediate call to action leading them to a specific offer

Disadvantages:

- Emails can carry viruses that can damage your computer system.
- Many companies attempt to send unwanted or unrequested email, commonly referred to as spam. Fortunately we're getting better software to filter it.
- It requires a lot of time and effort to build a substantial opt-in database. Without this database you have no one to send to.

People like getting emails from companies they trust. They are showing their approval by purchasing from companies who send them.

According to a 2009 study by Epsilon:

- 50 percent of those surveyed said they're more likely to buy products from companies who send them email, whether their purchases are online or at the place of business.
- In the retail category, 67 percent of respondents said they purchased products offline as a direct result of receiving an email from a retail company.

People who opt-in to your email marketing—those who willingly give you their email address—want your offers. They are begging for

Advertising

coupons and discounts, and frankly they enjoy the idea that they are part of an "exclusive club" of insiders who get deals nobody else is offered.

The best thing about these subscribers is they are your loyal customer base—the people who will come back time and again. And even if you send a coupon and they don't use it this month, you are directly tapping them on the shoulder to say, "Hi, we're still here, and we're still interested in being your favorite business."

Email Objectives

Typically there are three goals:

1. High number of impressions—a lot of people saw your ad. You've created *awareness*.
2. High number of clicks—you've generated enough *interest* that they now want to *evaluate* it further.
3. High number of Conversions—you're getting them to *respond* the way you intended.

Conversions

Conversions are getting your audience to do what you hoped they'd do. For instance, you don't want them to simply see your banner and leave. You want them to click on it, which normally takes them to a "landing page" with the details of the offer. The click was the conversion objective.

You can have more than one conversion objective in a sequence. Using the example above, when your prospect arrives at the landing page, you may ask them to fill out a form, place an order, click to start a chat with your business rep, etc. All of these are conversions.

Customer Retention with Email

Earlier I explained that the estimated cost of acquiring new customers is around ten-times higher than the cost to gain business from existing customers.

Previous customers already know you, where you're located, what you do, what you offer, etc. Unless they had a bad experience with you in the past, with a little prompting or reminding from you, they would be more likely to do business with you again rather than with somebody they've never met. Given the alternative of investing in advertising to reach a wide audience of people who don't know you, who probably aren't in the market at this time, and who already have some other business they're used to dealing with, doesn't it makes sense to invest some effort in *bringing back repeat* customers before you try to bring in new customers?

I had a client come in our office to discuss advertising, particularly mass media options. As the discussion began I asked, *"How long have you been in business?" "About 10 years,"* he replied. I then asked, *"How many customer records do you have?"* He answered, *"I probably have around 6,000."* My next question made him pause, *"When was the last time you invited them back?" "Well,"* he responded, slowly, *"I really haven't."*

Basically, instead of picking the low-lying fruit, he was ready to climb the tree to get to the fruit higher up.

Now this client has been and still is a very good businessman. He was quick to see the obvious potential he was overlooking, and our discussion turned toward developing an email campaign.

Email ROI

The ROI for a good email program can be impressive. Let's look at a typical example from a real customer:

A mid-size candy manufacturing company came to us looking for some help to increase online sales. They had a significant number of email addresses that they were sporadically messaging, but the emails didn't look like their website, and often focused on coupons that were valid for in-store purchases only.

Advertising

Here are the steps we took:

- We redesigned their email messages to match their brand and their website
- We created email offers that were good for online purchases in addition to, or instead of, in-store purchases
- We offered free shipping with a code that could be found only in the email
- We offered incentives for forwarding the email to friends and family

After a few months their subscribers re-engaged. Through consistent emails their online and in-store sales grew. In fact, their holiday online sales doubled over the previous year.

Database: 9,800 emails

Cost per email: $500

Cost per recipient: $0.051

Average email open rate: 28 percent (2,744 opens)

Average sale per opened email: $8

Total sales: $21,952

How to Create Emails

There are services such as Mail Chimp, Constant Contact and others that you can use to build your database, design your ads, send them and generate reports of measurement. The cost is minimal at around $9.95 a month.

There are three important areas of email you must understand and learn in order to get results.

- Relevance: the number one reason subscribers opt out of email is lack of relevance to them. If you can't craft a message that they find relevant, you lose them.
- Design: the second highest reason people opt out of email is lack of appeal. You can have a great offer, but if it looks bad, or if

people can't see your images, then you lose credibility and people will opt out.

- Database growth: the average email database loses 25 percent of subscribers each year through opt-out and/or changed email addresses. An experienced email marketing firm will be able to help you with tactics to grow your database and limit churn.

Opt-in vs. Spam

There are two primary types of email marketing, and you should ***only*** employ the opt-in method. The anti-spam laws are becoming very strict in the United States and even more so in Europe. Don't set yourself up for headaches by becoming a "spammer."

Opt-in

Company lists or databases are developed when there is some form of existing relationship between you and the prospect. They are sent only by opt-in request and permission, and anybody can opt-out at any time. They are normally welcomed by recipients with 14 percent-16 percent opened.

Opt-in lists are generally built from the following:

- Previous customers
- Vendors
- Business contacts
- Friends and family

Spam

Spam has become a serious problem in the email world. Every day we get offers, newsletters and hidden viruses from uninvited emails. Purchased or rented email lists very often contain "spam traps" that can ruin your email reputation and make it almost impossible to send legitimate emails in the future. In short, *"just say no"* to spam.

Purchased lists can be expensive and are often unreliable. Recipients are less receptive than opt-in lists you've created because there is no ex-

Advertising

isting relationship. The recipient considers contact to be an uninvited so-
licitation.

How to Grow Email Databases

You should make it a high priority to grow your database of customers and prospects. In every transaction you should attempt to collect their
email address so you can stay in touch with them. Here are a few ways to
do this:

1. Post a "Sign Up for Special Coupons" or "to get our Newsletter"
   on your website. Put a click link in a conspicuous place on the
   home page. Also, put offers on different pages of your website.
2. In all your traditional marketing or advertising, find ways to encourage this audience to sign up by going to a URL contact form,
   your website or Facebook page, or even using a QR code.
3. Send direct mail offers to previous clients offering them some
   incentive to go to a URL or your website and sign up.
4. Create an offer such as an eBook, whitepaper or coupon that requires your visitors to provide their email address to download
   them.
5. Hosting an online webinar is a good way to collect emails when
   attendees register. You could also co-host this with a partner to
   gain more signups.
6. Promote an online contest or give-away that requires an email
   address to enter.
7. Trade shows are a great place to collect addresses. Put a box for
   business cards or have them sign up to win a prize on a form that
   requires an email address.
8. Ask for current recipients to refer their friends and contacts. Setup
   a share button so they may easily forward your information, blog,
   coupon or newsletter to a friend or associate.
9. Put sign up tabs on your Facebook.

Marketing Survival in a Digital World

10. Promote an offer for a coupon on a Twitter campaign.
11. Pinterest is also an effective option to sign up clients.
12. Send an offer to Linked-In contacts. However, make sure it is relevant to the recipients or you may get in hot water with LinkedIn. Try to post your offer in relevant groups. Be sure to post a sign up offer on your LinkedIn Company Page.
13. Collaborating with other websites can be useful. For instance, if you've written an eBook, ask a relevant affiliate to post the sign up on their website.
14. If you have videos on YouTube, be sure to close with some call to action or links for them to sign up.
15. Google+ business page is another good source to post on to gain sign-ups.
16. Most of all ensure you have great content and valuable offers. Going through a lot of trouble to gain addresses won't matter if they opt out because what you delivered didn't meet your hype or their expectations.

Lead-In Offers

To get people to sign up, you need to give them something in exchange. The days of "Sign up for my newsletter" are gone. When it was novel, we'd do it. We were curious. What we got was inboxes full of irrelevant junk. This is the number one reason for opt-out.

Today very few will sign up without some sort of exchange. You need to have something of value to offer. Here are a few things that may interest them.

- On-line only coupons
- Blog bundled by topic
- Sharing data you've collected or studies you've conducted
- Presentation slides
- Audio or Webinars you produced

Advertising

- Interviews you've recorded
- Creating co-branded content helps
- Checklists
- FAQ's (Frequently Asked Questions)

Professional Email Services

This book is designed to teach you how to do much of your marketing yourself. In some areas, such as email or online, you may have learned what you need to do, but decide to seek out some professional assistance.

Direct Mail

Direct mail can be used to send postcards, letters, catalogs and circular offers to past customers or prospects. Mailing lists can be purchased or rented, but the most effective are lists of past customers or contacts—people you know are interested in your product. Direct mail is sent to customers based on criteria such as age, income, location, profession, buying pattern, etc. This is typically done by bulk mail that offers reduced rates over typical mailing costs.

A good tactic for using direct mail is to compel your previous and current customers to opt-in to your email newsletter or special online-coupon programs. Offer a "customer reward" for signing up to receive your emails—$5.00 off your next purchase, a free inspection, whatever is of value to get your past customers to give you an email address. Make some offers on-line only. You can start reaching them more frequently and cost-effectively through email, stop spending a lot of money on direct mail, and speak to them more often. Typically, you should plan on sending direct mail two or three times to encourage people to convert to your email program. Warn them that they will not be receiving mail from you anymore, and you'd be surprised how many people will make the switch.

Traditional direct mail can be costly, especially at today's postal rates. Design, printing, postage, and list rentals can all add up pretty quickly. Most studies show that the return on direct mail is down to an average half of 1 percent. We used to get an 8 percent return before it got overused. That's a lot of work and investment for not a lot of return.

When Should You Advertise?

Well, when do you need to get noticed? This can vary greatly depending on the nature of your product or service.

There is an old saying in advertising: "Shoot at the ducks when the ducks are flying." In other words, create exposure to match demand.

I classify demand periods three ways: Consistent, Situational and Seasonal

Consistent Demand

Consistent Demand applies to products or services with level demand and purchased year-round, i.e. milk, sugar, gasoline, clothes, etc.

With consistent demand you have a need to maintain a presence, based primarily on competition levels, of course. If you're the only grocery store within 25 miles, you probably don't need to advertise.

Consistent demand buying often turns into habits. Once someone gets accustomed to shopping a store for milk, or goes to one dentist for regular checkups, barring convenience and satisfaction, they tend to stay and repeat.

If convenience and satisfaction are equal, and you have a competitor who is advertising, the absence of your advertising will create a situation where you will probably lose customers and market share. In these circumstances you probably need to maintain a regular message to gain the advantage of being the first recalled.

Advertising

Top of Mind Awareness (TOMA)

Earlier I spoke about the power of branding to increase recall, and how the order in which your product or service is recalled increases the odds of being selected. Obviously, this creates a high value on keeping yourself positioned on the top of the consumer's brain through regular exposure and advertising.

In advertising, creating a position of easy recall is referred to as TOMA—Top Of Mind Awareness. It's simply finding a way to regularly stay on prospects' minds.

Regular, consistent contact is essential for creating TOMA, which helps you retain clients and/or acquire new ones. They must think of you often and think of you first.

This is why McDonald's and Ford and AT&T continue to spend bazillions of dollars in advertising. Everybody already knows who they are, but these companies understand that if they don't continue to advertise, after a while their competition will advertise their way into the public's mind to become the first one considered; and retaining ground is easier than gaining ground in market share.

Situational Demand

Situational Demand is products purchased more often based on emergency or circumstances. These might include snow-melt or snow shovels, bottled water and batteries, umbrellas, the need for a locksmith or an HVAC repair service, car batteries, etc.

The Thin Market Rule

The Thin Market Rule states that "people are only in the market for a limited time. When they are, you must be on *"the top of their mind."*

Most people are not perpetually looking for tires, plumbing fixtures, clothes, automobiles, books, lawyers, dentists, musical instruments, computers, pets, garden supplies, furniture, reading glasses, etc. In our lifetime, while we might use all these things, we generally only shop for them when the need arises.

- The retail market on any given day is very thin. Only 4 percent of all adults will buy the average retail product in a given week.
- Half of your business is into the market and out again in seven days. Typically, customers will actively seek advertising to help them with their buying decision within a seven-day period. You want to reach those customers the week they are buying.

A few months back, I noticed one of my tires was getting bald. Prior to that, I completely tuned out all advertising concerning tires (and anything else I wasn't actively in the market for). But from the moment I needed a new set, I paid close attention to every television and newspaper ad I saw concerning tires. I wanted the ads to educate me about the features and benefits of different brands, and any specials retailers were offering.

I went to visit a dealer that advertised a good, brand name tire for a good price and I bought the set. Once the tires were installed and I drove away from the shop, I stopped paying attention to tire advertisements.

So who made the sale? It was the retailer who had an offer precisely when I needed it. How did the advertiser know when that was? He probably didn't. He just knew he had to keep his message out there until I was ready.

This is how TOMA applies to situational demand. Most situational needs are unpredictable and may require you to maintain a consistent advertising presence.

Seasonal Demand

Seasonal Demand products have predictable high and low demand periods—sometimes referred to as spikes.

Advertising

While it's possible to have all three, most tend to have one or maybe two demand characteristics.

For instance:

- People buy eggs on a fairly normal basis through the year (consistent), but there is much more demand during Easter or other holidays (seasonal).
- Clothes are purchased through the year (consistent), but demand spikes prior to back to school and Christmas (seasonal).
- Some folks have their HVAC serviced regularly (seasonal), but if their ac suddenly goes out they need a technician immediately (situational).

Seasonal Budgeting

There is an old saying: *"When things are slow you need to advertise."* While I believe in the value and power of advertising, this statement is a bit oversimplified. Do you think a company selling swimming pools will sell lots of pools in Missouri during December just because they advertise? Not unless they're giving the pools away. This same pool dealer will get a far better rate of return on their advertising dollars starting their campaign as people begin to thaw out and the weather starts turning warmer.

Again, this is why I prefer the strategy: "Shoot at the ducks when the ducks are flying." Rather than spending a lot of money trying to convince people to do what they normally wouldn't, save your cash and use it to get more of the people when they're ready.

Here are some simple steps you can take to maximize your advertising return based on normal sales levels.

Marketing Survival in a Digital World

Step 1. Let's start by identifying Gross Sales by month

We can see substantial changes in sales volume across the year. To make it easier, look at the sales by quarter:

1st QTR	12 %
2nd QTR	55 %
3rd QTR	31 %
4th QTR	2 %

If the advertising budget for this business was around $60,000 per year, do you think it makes sense to allocate $5,000 evenly across the whole year? Of course not.

Step 2—Allocate your advertising dollars spent by your gross sales.

If your annual advertising budget was $60,000:

	Quarterly Sales		Advertising
1st QTR	12 %	$7,338	12% of $60,000
2nd QTR	55 %	$32,700	55% of $60,000
3rd QTR	31 %	$18,786	31% of $60,000
4th QTR	2 %	$1,174	2% of $60,000 – or reallocate

Now you've invested the money at times you're most likely to have buyers.

Step 3—Adjust to match decision interest and evaluation timing

Most products and services, especially higher cost items, are not impulse buys. People start planning sometime in advance before they sign the bottom line. In this case, if we know that pool buyers usually consider a pool two months before they buy, we might want to shift advertising allocation forward by maybe 30 days. So, after they've spent their first month talking themselves into a pool, you're right there over the next 30 days to convince them to buy from you.

Now, if this same pool retailer also sold fireplace inserts, he may have more of an evenly-spaced allocation, but his message would need to change as his selling seasons change. While this seems like a simple concept, you'd be surprised how many businesses just run the same message all year long, regardless of seasonal product and service changes.

Stimulation & Relevance

If you're looking for a lot of discussion of creative in this book, you're out of luck. The creative process is too vast and too subjective to confine to a chapter. It requires an entire book on its own. So let's stick with more scientific aspects.

To create both awareness and interest you need to "attract" them though a stimulus. You must also immediately "engage" them through something that is relevant to them.

Stimulants

The higher a stimulation an advertisement presents, the greater the awareness.

According to the research of Walker and Dubinsky:

"Even without science, one would agree that if people like an advertisement, they are more likely to notice and to pay attention to it and are in-turn more likely to assimilate and respond to the message it offers."

Marketing Survival in a Digital World

The journal of management and marketing research released a study, "Circadian Rhythms and Their Effects on Advertising Recall," which demonstrated the effect of the stimulus. The study showed over a two week period, what stimulated younger people seeing ads.

Study time	9:00 a.m.		3:30 p.m.		overall results	
Humor	67	29.8 %	99	27.1 %	166	56.9 %
Creative ad	41	18.2 %	27	7.4 %	68	25.6 %
Vivid image	32	14.2 %	77	21.1 %	109	35.3 %
Irritating	22	9.8 %	24	6.6 %	46	16.4 %
Emotional appeal	12	5.3 %	11	3.0 %	23	8.3 %
Brand familiarity	11	4.9 %	17	7.4 %	28	12.3 %
Music in ad	9	4.0 %	14	3.8 %	23	7.8 %
Unsure	8	3.6 %	15	4.1 %	23	7.7 %
Previously viewed	7	3.1 %	23	6.3 %	30	9.4 %
Exposure repetition	6	2.7 %	9	2.5 %	15	5.1 %
Celebrity in ad	4	1.8 %	10	2.7 %	14	4.5 %
Sex appeal	3	1.3 %	7	1.9 %	10	3.3 %
Other	2	0.9 %	32	8.8 %	34	9.7 %
Like the brand	1	0.4 %	0	0.0 %	1	0.4 %

Note the top two reasons for recall account for 48.2 percent of the overall reasons for recall: humor and creative. Younger people respond to an entertainment stimulus. However, one stimulus does not fit all.

Although it typically has a younger demographic, in the retail engagement ring business, funny doesn't sell. In fact, the product itself is not total stimulus. Brides-to-be are stimulated by the "romantic experience" of the selection process (shopping) almost as much as the ring itself. They want to see style, elegance, love, and personal attention within jewelry store advertisements.

Advertising

Ad Stimulation by Gender

Many years ago I attended a marketing seminar in New York presented by some of the nation's largest and leading advertising agencies. One presentation I found particularly interesting was how different genders respond to advertising.

The presenter started by pointing out that women were better at multi-tasking than men. She credited this to evolution, clear back to the cave-days. During this time men had three tasks: procreate, protect and hunt. Women had far more responsibilities. They had to procreate, raise the children, make the clothes, harvest the food, make the meals, provision the house, etc. You can see the same behavior in most primitive tribes.

As a result, men developed very few multi-tasking skills while women learned how to hold a conversation between six others and understand every word.

The presenter then moved onto how these differences pertain to advertising. She told us she would show two advertisements that were the most successful at selling pants; one to males and the other for females.

The first thing I noticed about the female print ad shown was that it didn't show any pants; just a series of wispy cartoon-like illustrations of a young woman with red hair, a white shirt wearing some Gloria Vanderbilt jeans. She was depicted going to work, picking flowers, holding a child, doing summersaults, etc. There were also three long paragraphs of text.

While I thought this was some sort of joke, all the women around me were smiling and nodding their head in approval. The ad connected with them. It showed them an empowered woman in business, free and spirited; all the things they want. They also liked the story that went with it. Women like to read a lot more copy in advertising than men.

Next, she showed the print ad that sold pants to men. It was a black and white photograph of six men from the waist down, facing forward. The only copy on the ad said "Docker Jeans. Great fit. Good price."

To me, this made sense. Good fit and price are important. I see the jeans and I like the look. That's all I'd need to see to go investigate. The advertising agency knew this is the stimulus guys needed. And the reason for the black and white photo was because color confuses men.

Great thought should be put behind the creative and messaging stimulus when designing your advertising. You really have to go back to the psychographics discussed earlier in customer profiling to learn as much about your prospects as you can, then design your ads to stimulate your particular target as best you can.

Distracting Stimulants

We all know that the more entertaining or engaging an advertisement, the more people are going to notice it. The problem is when the stimulation to attract goes too far. An element that catches the attention or interest of a target audience can often become a distraction from the message. The objective of the ad is compromised and that makes the ad ineffective.

An example can be given from a study carried out by Tsai & Chang using female and male undergraduates to find out the effect of physical attractiveness of models on advertising effectiveness.

The study showed that the use of highly attractive models in ads resulted in a decrease in the ads effectiveness compared to using normally attractive models. **It was simply a case where the more stunning talent outshined the product. The distraction was too much.**

Nothing can sell if they don't pay attention. You must achieve Awareness. But you must also work to keep a balance in your advertising that promotes the process of moving viewers beyond Awareness and into Interest and Evaluation.

Advertising

Relevance

Relevance is one of the two factors that are predictive of new product success (Olson cited in "Du Plessis").

"The audience needs to believe that the ad is relevant to them if they are going to process the ad in the first place. Having an element of liking in advertisement might not be important if it cannot present a superior, relevant reason at the time the target audience intends to take an action relative to the intended message and objective of the ad."

Basically, if what you are doesn't matter to them, you're wasting your money.

I don't recall where I first heard or read this statement, but I believe it is one of the most important rules in preparing effective advertising:

"The message must put the desire of the potential customer before the advertiser's desire."

I know I covered this earlier, but it's worth repeating: It's not about what you need or want to sell. The message must be solely about what the customer needs or wants to buy.

Business owners tend to build their advertising in an ego-centric point of view. Most advertisers still lead-off about themselves.

- We've been in business for 50 years!
- We've got a great selection!
- Our service is second to none!
- Our goal is to always exceed expectations! Etc.

As a consumer, these may be important, but they're not what are most important. And what is most important is what matters to me!

Imagine you visit a car dealership to find a new ride, and the salesperson walk up to you and says:

"Hi, I'm Larry Smith! I've been the top salesperson here at XYZ Motors for the last three years. I've been working here since 2004 and I really know my stuff. I have lots of satisfied customers and I'm..."

Right about here you're asking yourself: *"Who is this guy? I'm not here to learn about him! What about me? I'm the customer!"*

Bad advertising behaves the same way as Larry Smith. It's always about them. Some never even address the consumer issues at all. They seem convinced that if they brag about themselves long enough, people will buy from them.

When most people examine an advertisement (or a website), the priority is "me first."

- Do "I" need this?
- Does this fit "my" needs?
- Is this easy for "me"?
- What is this going to cost "me"? Etc.

Shoppers are investing their time reviewing your ad to find something they want. Until they do, your company's history or wonderful qualities are not really important to them.

Beginning your relationship by talking about you is like yanking on the hook before a fish has taken the bait. Unfortunately many advertisers believe if they keep talking about themselves, their wants and needs long enough, and often enough consumers will fall in love with them. It just doesn't work that way.

Pre-Placement Evaluation

Pre-placement is trying to project a media's effectiveness and value based on numbers provided by third party entities such as **Nielsen** (television ratings), **Arbitron** (radio ratings) and **ABC- Audit Bureau of Circulation** (newsprint and magazines). These entities exist to collect data and provide unbiased and unexaggerated reports regarding different media's audience size and composition.

Advertising

I won't try to explain details of each entity. I will however explain some of the data they provide that you'll need to understand to project and compare different media options.

Audience Composition

Traditional and online media audiences can generally be broken down into groups of similar demographics or interest profiles.

Single Demographic Media

Some media have a singular or very narrow audience demographic. For instance, hip hop station listeners are young (at this time), Auto Week magazine primarily appeals to men, Better Homes & Gardens to middle-aged woman, Senior Living, well, you get the point. You buy that particular media because they have the audience you are trying to reach.

Multi-Demographic Media

Other media have multiple demographic audiences. Television demographics are based on the shows, not the station (except on cable where the viewers are always similar, like a radio station). One given television station may have seniors watching "The Price is Right," women watching "The View," men watching "Meet The Press" or children watching cartoons. The one station has uniquely different audiences at different times of the day.

You typically buy placement on particular shows that have your target demographic.

Newspapers act more like television stations in that they have a wide audience, different demographics tend to read only certain sections.

This is why specific-placement or "spot buys" are most common on multi-demographic media. We'll discuss this more under Media Allocation.

Impressions

An "impression" is a term used for measurement of exposure to something. In advertising it means your prospect has been *exposed* to the advertisement by sight or sound a given number of times.

If an owl hoots three times in the woods within your earshot, you received three hoot Impressions. If you see a cat in your front yard when you leave home, that's one Impression. If the cat is there when you come home, the cat has made *two* Impressions on you in one day.

Impressions are used as a common denominator when comparing the reach of one media vs. another. For instance, (using the city transportation department's numbers) a billboard company can say that during a day 32,532 cars drive down the street. So if they have a billboard located on that street, it should have 32, 532 Impressions per day (and you could further factor in the average number or riders in each car, etc.)

Here's how you apply this data: now let's say another billboard company has a billboard on another street that has 40,114 cars per day, and this company is asking the same monthly rent as the other billboard company is asking for the billboard that gets only 32,532 Impressions. You'd select the one with the most Impressions for the lowest cost per impression.

Cost Per Impression

One method a media buyer uses is called Cost Per Impression, or CPI.

If Nielsen studies show that one television show reaches 15,000 people one time per day, you could use the same math to compare the billboard CPI against that of the TV.

Using this common denominator (with all other considerations being equal), a media buyer can select the media that delivers *the most Impres-*

Advertising

sions for the lowest cost when comparing completely different types of media options, i.e. TV, cable, radio, etc.

Of course, this alone should not be the sole decision factor. Different media/mediums have different characteristics that must also be taken into consideration. CPI is just one of several.

Here is something that you need to remember about Impressions:

- Impressions are not the count of individuals, only the amount of exposures any given number of people could have had. In exaggerated terms, you could have 100,000 Impressions that were only seen by 10 people.

- Just because you are exposed to something doesn't mean you're paying attention to it. An Impression is not a guarantee that it *made* an impression. It just means the prospect was in the vicinity.

- Also important: your message has to reach the *right audience* to be effective. You won't sell many skateboards placing an ad in a senior's magazine, and you won't sell much knitting yarn on a hunting channel.

Reach & Frequency

Reach

Reach refers to the number of individuals within your target market that are exposed to a specific ad over a specific period of time. This number is expressed as a percentage of your total market.

Reach is often coupled with Frequency to establish an advertising campaign objective. Let me quickly explain Frequency and then the relation between the two.

Frequency

Frequency is the number of times individuals within your marketing area will be exposed to your ads during a given period of time. This is the average number of Impressions each will receive.

Remember the Wharton School of Business study that determined results increased with repetition? Obviously, the more someone hears your name the more likely they are to remember it. Conversely, the more times you are *exposed* to an advertisement, the more likely you are to remember it and pay attention to it. More Impressions *put the odds in your favor.*

Equally important to the number of Impressions is the length of time over which you receive them. One of the most annoying things I've seen inexperienced (or unethical) media reps do, is dazzle potential advertisers with a flyer showing that his/her annual media campaign will deliver 30 Impressions at a very low cost per impression.

What they fail to explain (because their sales manager failed to explain to them) is that, unless it's a memorable super-bowl ad, 30 Impressions over a 12-month span are probably next to worthless.

People only remember advertising messages for a few hours to a few days. So unless you've got Clydesdale horses playing football, don't be impressed by the low price.

Normally, we like to measure Frequency in 30-day increments. This is because most buyer and behavior studies about advertising use this time frame. As comparison studies go, it is our most common denominator of time.

Relation of Reach & Frequency

Typically, the more people a given media will reach, the more expensive it becomes. Remember I said you are *buying audience.* The more you buy, the higher the price.

Advertising

Reaching a lot of prospects is great, but as I said earlier, they have to see you quite a few times before they will notice or remember you. This is where you try to find a balance between the Reach and Frequency.

Let's say I want to put my ad on TV and I have a budget of $2,000. One highly popular TV show reaches 40,000 of my target audience but costs $2,000 per spot; there goes my budget for one Impression!

Typically people need to see your ad more than once to be motivated to purchase. There is an old advertising rule of thumb that states the magic number is 10. The number of times commonly accepted in media buying range between 3 to 10 exposures/Impressions within a 30-day period. Basically, seeing it one time isn't going to be enough to even make them aware you exist.

I tend to believe the number of Impressions required to attract and compel is more on the high side. Remember back in the branding chapter I stated that people don't like change. More often we prefer to stick with what we know unless we find we must make a change. Unless you're introducing a new product or there is high pent-up demand, I believe you're going to need to make more in the neighborhood of 12 Impressions.

There is a rule of thumb I use when calculating the Frequency needed for local network television:

Awareness: 3-4 Impressions

- Remember the competition for attention I spoke of earlier? You're going to need to have a number of exposures to cut through the clutter and get noticed.

Interest: 3-4 Impressions

- After they've taken a little notice, you need to keep driving the message in front of them so they finally commit to listen to you.

Evaluations: 3-4 Impressions

- Now you need to keep the pressure to reinforce your credibility and get them to investigate and eventually move into acceptance.

When should you see sales?

For local network buys, a common goal is to reach at least 50 percent of your target demographic with a *minimum* of four Impressions per month. If you need a total of 10 Impressions, it will take around three months to convince them.

Impression impact value

The number of Impressions required may vary depending on the impact of the Impression (the delivery). Television has visual that helps to demonstrate. For radio, you often need far more Frequency.

A common radio goal is to reach 10 percent of your target with a minimum of 4 to 6 Impressions per week. This would imply a typical radio ad has about a quarter of the impression value as a local television spot. I would probably agree. Radio always seems to require a saturation to show measurement. I have nothing more to base that on other than personal experience.

If this theory holds true, you need to consider that you shouldn't pay more than 25 percent for radio than you do for local network television with decent ratings. On the other hand, the production cost of the TV can reduce the gap closer to half.

Ratings

In broadcast media, ratings are used to help you measure audience size of a particular show.

A rating point is 1 percent of the households with TV, within a geographical area. This could be used to measure audience nationally, regionally and/or even within a city limit.

Imagine your DMA has 30 counties and there are 1,000,000 households with TVs. If **Nielsen** reported a particular network's evening news

Advertising

achieved a rating of 5, this means 5 percent of the TV households tune in to that show. Your audience would be 50,000 viewers.

Basically, the more rating points a show has, the bigger the audience and reach. More ratings are a good thing.

Cost Per Point

What you pay for a rating point will vary from show to show, and station to station. There is not a fixed price. Generally, if a show is very popular, or it usually sells out faster, it will cost you more per rating point than a rating for a show that is less popular or has unsold inventory.

Media buyers use a measurement call Cost Per Point (CPP) to compare the value of the rating to what is being charged.

If you have two shows that meet your demographic audience target, one with a CPP of $12 and the other with a CPP of $10, you're probably wiser to choose the lower. This is particularly more useful when comparing station to station rates.

Sometimes the best option is to pick the second-best show and buy more ads rather than to run only one ad in the best show. Naturally you want to buy all the ratings points you can, but you must be careful to balance the Reach with the Frequency. You don't want to buy just one show with a huge audience—remember the Frequency repetition required?

For example, if Oprah pulls 5 percent of the audience during her time frame, but one ad costs you $500, you might be able to afford only one ad per week during her show. If Ellen pulls 3 percent of the audience and costs $250 per ad, you may do better buying two ads for the same money and reach the same audience more frequently.

Gross Rating Point

GRPs (Gross Rating Points) is the total amount of ratings (audience) you are purchasing in a given time period. These are grouped for the purpose of evaluating a total campaign's effectiveness based on the total rating points. These totals are then compared to established benchmarks.

Let's say Oprah pulls a rating (percent of the available audience) of 5 every day of the week. Each time you place an ad in Oprah, you are buying 5 ratings points. If you purchase an ad in Oprah five days a week for four weeks (20 times total) you are purchasing 100 GRPs (20 ads x 5 rating points per ad).

After determining all the combined ratings from all the shows you're buying over the campaign life, the media buyer would then compare that total against the established benchmarks. The less GRPs you run, the weaker your exposure value.

Typically they look like this on an average 30-day period:

GRPs	Effective Rating
200 – 300	weak
301 – 500	moderate
501 – 800	aggressive
801 +	very aggressive

Often you want to consider not just a show's rating points, but its effective rating points. These are the ratings of only those which will reach the audience most likely to purchase from you. If you buy advertising on a station that has a wide area reach, you might want to only look at ratings within your Metro area. Of course, you need to consider the fact that online has reduced geographical consideration if you can deliver to their home, so more ratings in outlying areas are now more effective.

Share

A share is the percentage of all the people who are actually viewing television during a 30-minute period of time, or listening to a radio during a 15-minute period of time. For instance, if 100,000 people are

Advertising

watching their televisions at 6:00 p.m., and 25,000 are watching Channel 3, then Channel 3 has a 25 percent share (of active viewers).

Share is actually more useful than ratings. You can't force people to view the television, but having the lion's share of those who actually view is the objective of competing media.

Media Buying Agencies

The data discussed above can normally be obtained from each individual media, or through an advertising agency you hire. You cannot simply contact **Nielsen** or **Arbitron** to obtain this information. It is supplied as a subscription.

You can normally trust the information even when coming from a media that would like to sell you some advertising. The liability for altering this data is severe.

I would recommend you always retain a media buying agency to handle this for you. In most cases (media), it won't cost you anything because most media has been priced with a 15 percent agency commission in their rate. You are charged this regardless if you have an agency handle it or you do it yourself.

The bulk of advertising placed with a media normally comes to them from advertising agencies. So they priced their buys accordingly. As an agency I can buy the same spot you pay $100 for only $85. This is called Gross Pricing. As an advertiser, you cannot normally get the media to discount the 15 percent if you choose to do it yourself because that would not set well with their primary customers (agencies).

Sometimes the media is Net Priced, meaning there is no built-in 15% agency fee. If you hire an agency to place it for you, they will need to add their commission on top. They use a factor of 17.65 to "gross it up" and achieve a 15% commission.

Either way, I think it is still a great value. An agency will know better how to assemble your media campaign, give you unbiased recommendations, place the media for you, and even check the media invoices to ensure they are accurate.

It's easy to see wisdom in paying 15 percent or even 17.65% more than it would cost you to an agency for the service and the potential to get far more value from your advertising dollars.

Media placement

Determine Best Media Options

So now you've done your research and you've found some good media options to try, you should identify the best potential 3 to 5 media choices. Here are some examples of what you should consider.

- Which media provides the lowest cost to reach our target demographic based on a cost per 1,000 basis?
- Does it provide acceptable Reach and Frequency levels based on that particular type of media?
- Does the medium have the right delivery means? In other words, do I need a media with visual to demonstrate? Would the limited message ability of a billboard work well? Is my audience outside, the home where the radio would be the best choice?
- Are we able to apply these only with known seasonal demand? For example, what if a swimming pool company had to pay for a billboard year-round?

There are many more questions you need to ask yourself. Again, advice from an unbiased media buyer would be greatly beneficial to help you determine and examine all these considerations.

Advertising

Start With Single Media Placement

I strongly recommend you test one media at a time before building a multi-media campaign. If you use more than one at a time, you probably won't be able to determine which performed best.

By isolating each media within the same market, with the same offer, in a similar time period, with the same budget, you'll be able to see which tend to cause more engagement in post-placement evaluation.

Multi-Media Allocation

After you have tested all your best media options, you might want to consider a multi-media campaign.

The odds of creating awareness increase dramatically when applied simultaneously across multiple traditional and digital media channels with a unified message.

A recent study by Ipsos demonstrated when one media form, such as television, is combined with other touch points, such as radio or print, ad recall can exponentially increase.

Cross-promoting can make it seem like your product is everywhere, improving brand awareness and recall.

Spot Buy/Rotation/Day part

Spot Buy

Spot buys are when you select exactly where you want your ad to appear. It may be a particular television show, or only a cover position in a magazine or a certain section in the newspaper.

Spot buys are most often used in multi-demographic media. Do you remember the discussion earlier regarding the fact that the viewing audience can change radically depending on the show, or that different audiences prefer (and read) different sections of a newspaper? You would certainly need control to ensure your ad in the right place at the right time to be seen by the right audience.

Rotation Buys

Rotation buys are when you allow the station to select where your ads run. This gives them flexibility and the chance to sell you unsold inventory. In exchange, they deeply discount the spots. Rotation buys are most often used in single demographic media and are a good tool to gain Frequency.

Rotation buys are usually packaged; many spots are sold as a group. You will normally get good spots and not so good spots. While it may look like you're getting a ton of spots, you may be overpaying. You need to take a look at what you're paying for effective reach.

I had one client that was feeling pretty good about his negotiations with the radio station. He had purchased 400 spots per month in a rotation buy at a CPM (Cost Per 1,000) of $10, when the average rate was more around $15.

After reviewing his buy I found that 50 percent of his ads ran overnight and in time periods so low that they didn't even register a listening audience. So effectively he was paying $20 CPM because only half were being heard.

If your rotation includes a lot of spots where nobody is watching or listening (low ratings), you should pay a deeply discounted price for the package.

Day Part

Day part is used for broadcast to determine what time to run your ads. They are short ranges of times that tend to have similar programs, characteristics and/or audience composition. They are sort of a small rotator within a short time period.

Advertising

In radio you might have morning drive, lunch, evening drive, and other. In television you have morning news, early fringe, prime time, late fringe, overnight, etc.

When you place an ad by day part, you're saying I want my ad to run somewhere during morning drive (between 6:00 a.m. and 9:00 a.m.) rather than saying you want it to run at 8:45 a.m.

5

WEBSITES

Today the website is the hub of all marketing and advertising. If you don't currently have a good website—or any website—make that your Number 1 priority. Yes, it's that important. According to the 2008 online conversion report, *"Eighty-six percent of people research a company online before choosing whether or not to use them."* So if you don't have a good website, you're losing business, and probably a lot more than you think. Remember, this is one of the first places we go to Evaluate.

People go to your website to learn:
- What you do or what you offer
- Where you're located or when you're open
- Shop or compare your prices to competitors
- Assess your professionalism (presentation)
- Research your reputation

The degree of research varies by product, and by age groups. Studies have shown an average of 15 percent to 30 percent will use the Internet to research a mechanic; the highest majority in the 18-25 year range. An average of 50 percent to 60 percent of people will use the Internet to research consumer electronics before they buy them.

Think about how this applies to your own buying behavior. When you bought that 60" plasma TV, you researched them online first to discover reasonable pricing, which brand was rated best by experts, and what other buyers had to say.

According to Google, *"Current and potential customers will judge your business by your website. Fair or not, it will happen. If your site has problems, you are very likely losing customers as a direct result."*

Website MCD

As online has grown, it has created more complexity in marketing communication; particularly in the emergence of a phenomenon I've labeled "Marketing Component Dependencies" or "MCD" for short.

MCD is a condition where the absence or poor performance of one or more critical marketing communication component can substantially reduce or even negate the performance of all the rest of your advertising and/or communication efforts. Think of it like a chain with a broken link

Around 2003, we started noticing a trend. Certain clients who had a long history of consistent sales were now experiencing a slow-down for no apparent reason. (This was before the recession of 2009, when the winds of economic prosperity blew so hard that even chickens could fly.)

The more we tried to determine why their sales had slowed, the more we were confused. We examined the five "usual suspects," but there was nothing obviously out of place.

The Usual Suspects

1. **Demand:** They had market demand for their product or service
2. **Offer:** They had a good offer
3. **Advertising:** They had sufficient advertising budget (even with fragmentation)

Websites

4. **Reputation:** They had a good reputation
5. **Competition**: The competition wasn't doing anything to outflank them

Over a short time, we noticed the same issue develop with other clients. Marketing folks started calling others to explain the situation only to find many of their clients' also had the same issue. After many tests and a little more time, we found the common denominator: all the advertisers with slowing sales had a lousy website or no website at all.

As I said, historically we have always depended on our advertising to create Awareness, Interest and Evaluation. After seeing the advertising they were now looking for the advertiser's websites to Evaluate. Clients who didn't have a website, or those with a website looked like the back of a cereal box didn't pass the grade. Thus, the Evaluations didn't occur and sales didn't either.

When the slow-down first began the clients blamed the usual goat: the advertising. But when we built or replaced a client's website with a better one – *miraculously; the advertising started working again.*

This is now the norm rather than the exception. Today, 78 percent of all shoppers use the Internet to research and purchase products and services. In essence, consumers will research a company online before making the decision to do business with them, so if you don't have a good website, you might as well stop advertising and save your advertising money until you build a good one.

Here's something else to consider: if you are advertising on traditional media, and people are going to the Internet to try to find your website, but you don't have one or it's bad—where do you think they are taking their business? ***Directly to your competitor who has a good website.. You have spent money on advertising your competitor's business.*** Because of this, I recommend businesses pull their advertising until they have a proper website in place.

What Your Website Must Do

The primary function of the website is to ***Engage and Convert*** visitors. Just like in your brick and mortar store, the longer a prospect stays, the more they learn about your services, thereby increasing the odds for a sale.

Today, most people browsing leave a website within 10 seconds. Why? They don't find anything immediately relevant or of value to them. They are becoming less inclined to read through several paragraphs to investigate you. This increases your bounce rate, and a high bounce rate is bad. If you don't engage them, and get them to investigate more about your product or services—you lose the sale.

Conversion simply means, "What do you want them to do when they visit your site?" What is the goal? Do you want them to fill out a form, or subscribe to your newsletter? Do you want them to buy from you online, give you a phone call or email you? By knowing the end goal, you'll create a better design that leads and compels them to that path. You then set goals for yourself to try to increase conversions.

As Important As Your Store

You have one chance to make a first impression. Buying those "one size fits all" do-it-yourself website templates that look like the back of a cereal box is not going to save you money. It will cost you money. Spend some money and time to make your website dazzle your prospects, so it will help you make sales.

Website Design and Development

There are three critical components in a high-quality website:
1. Design
2. Development
3. Strategy

Websites

Most websites are created with only one, maybe two, of these elements intact. Only the best websites address all three, and if you want your website to be better than your competitor's website, you need to be sure yours has all three elements.

When you're looking for help with your website, remember to look for someone who not only has experience, but success stories and satisfied customers who can attribute sales and increased traffic to their website. You need a designer, a developer, and a strategist on your website team. Normally, a designer and developer are two different people; one more right brain and the other more left. You might occasionally find a designer who has development experience—they are rare and highly coveted! My advice is to hire a website group that has both.

And this is very, very important: Make sure your website is built to be mobile friendly. More than half of all website visits are done on a mobile phone. If your website looks good on a personal computer, it may not be viewable on an iPhone. You should consider building in html5 or something that will make your site "responsive." This means it will adjust to a smaller screen (like an iPhone) to make it simpler to read.

6

SEARCH ENGINE MARKETING

Search Engine Marketing involves the promotion of website visits by increasing their visibility through Search Engine Optimization and online advertising.

This is an important disclaimer: By the time you read this, something online has changed. Online communications, tools and trends are changing so fast, the only way you can stay abreast is by monitoring online studies and reports, blogs and such. I now begin every day looking at new studies and reports explaining the latest and greatest online applications.

The only thing I can say is, to the best of my knowledge, within a 10 second period of time the following information was reasonably accurate (as far as I am aware).

Position is Important

A critical goal to get evaluated is to "direct" as many prospects to your website as you can. To do this, you must be positioned high on the search engine results.

As time went on, another MCD developed. A couple of years after the dawn of mandatory websites, it became apparent we now had to improve how we "direct" people to those websites when they browse. We entered the world of another MCD called SEO – Search Engine Optimization.

SEO is the process of improving your websites position (ranking) when you enter keywords into a search engine such as Google. Where your website is positioned on a Search Engine Results Page (SERP) is critical. You need to be at or near the top.

Recent studies by Cornell University and New York University showed that 88 percent of people browsing with a search engine will only consider the first five companies listed before changing the keyword search. So, if you're not one of the first five, you're toast. In fact, if they browsed after seeing your advertisements, you've spent money to provide your competitors with more prospective business.

Some business owners with poor positioning have asked "What if I advertise more? Will they be more likely to shop for me by name?" Probably not. They will still more often search by product or what they want than by your name. The extra advertising you buy will probably make your situation worse.

Remember, advertising makes people Aware of a product or service and creates Interest, which leads them to Evaluation. When you advertise, you're getting them all worked up to seek the product you're promoting as much as you are promoting yourself. Since most people still search by the product or service, you're simply paying to deliver more prospects into the hands of your competitors who have better search engine position than you do. Your problem compounds itself and you're actually paying to drive yourself out of business.

So first you had to get a website or your prospects wouldn't make a commitment. Then, you had to improve your SERP positioning through

SEO applications. Now, you'll also need a blog to improve your popularity and visits in order to help your SEO position, etc. Like adding links in a chain, the list of Marketing Component Dependencies continues to grow. The expanding role social marketing and mobile communications play in the chain require you to incorporate those into your campaigns if you want to stay competitive.

Most Keyword Searches Are By Product

Most people search by entering keywords for *the product or service they're interested in* rather than a specific store name. For instance, if someone in Springfield wants to buy flowers, they will enter "florist Springfield MO" more often than "Mary's Flower Shop."

This is typical for new prospects. They may have no particular loyalty to a store. So they enter a keyword product or service to see who and how many others provide the same so they compare them side-by-side (usually on price).

While there is a better chance a previous customer will search for you by name, more and more are putting loyalty aside to see if they can find a better deal through comparison shopping.

Remember, the first five websites listed are usually the only ones who are really evaluated. Unless you are in this Top 5, investing more in advertising will actually work against you. You're just leading more prospects to your competitors who are listed higher.

Dynamic Search

More traditional search results are moving from the traditional text listings such as organic results and toward dynamic content like map listings, reviews on Google Properties and Google Carousel. I would suggest you Google these to find their current applications since they are still in the development stage at the time of this writing.

SEM Components

Browsers

When you go online to "surf" (look around), you generally start by opening up a web browser. A web browser is a software application that retrieves and presents information to you from resources on the World Wide Web. This can include websites, video, images or other content.

The major web browsers today are Google Chrome, Firefox, Internet Explorer and Safari.

Google is the largest receiving over 68 percent of all browser requests. Bing will soon be the default or only search available for Siri on the new IOS or Apple products, so the numbers could change drastically in the very near future. But for the following examples, we're going to stick with Google.

Search Engines

To begin, you open Google and you'll see a box in the middle of the page. Believe it or not, these little boxes are called search engines. I'm still trying to figure out why they didn't call them search boxes?

Keywords

To operate the search engine you enter in a query (words, names or phrases) of something you want to display. The words you enter are called "keywords" or "keyword phrases."

For instance, if you wanted to research George Washington you'd type his name in the search engine and boom, up would come a page (search engine results page or SERP) with all kinds of information about George.

Search Engine Results Page (SERP)

Across the top of the SERP you'll see links where you could view pictures of George or video's featuring George, or maps that show you where George slept, along with a list of many websites that have information on George.

The SERP page typically contains:
- Organic listings (of websites)
- Paid-positioned websites commonly referred to as PPC (Pay Per Click). On Google these are normally the top two or three placed on a light yellow background, plus all the website listings down the far right column. The owners of these sites paid Google to position them here because they probably don't have a high enough organic (earned) position on the page.
- You many also see bullet point listings down below the first five. These are called a "Directory Listing" or "Google Places." You want to be here too. You will also start seeing Carousel for some searches.

SEO - Search Engine Optimization

Search engine optimization is the process of improving organic (earned) search results within search engines such as Google, Yahoo and Bing just to name a few.

Positioning Is Critical

A few years ago, you could be listed on page two and still get some traffic to visit you. You would have a 75 percent chance of a visit if you were anywhere on Page 1, a 20 percent chance if you were on Page 2 and even a 5 percent chance if you were on Page 3.

As search engines continued to refine relevant displays based on keywords entered, people realized that if they didn't find what they were looking for on the first page, they would just enter new keywords or keyword phrases rather than search more pages.

As I stated earlier, a study by Cornel University and New York University claims, 88 percent of people will only click on the top five listings before entering in new keywords in the browser.

Today, if your business is not at or near the top of the first page and within the first five websites displayed, you're losing business to competitors that out-position you.

Placement positioning is the new battleground. And the process you employ to improve your positioning is called Search Engine Optimization or SEO.

The Search Engine Provider's Objectives

The mission of search engines (Google, MSN, Yahoo, etc.) is to provide searchers (their customers) with the most "relevant" result to their query.

How Search Engines Determine Results

Search engines use a complex and constantly evolving process that involves algorithms combined with many other factors to determine relevance.

One factor in the process that reviews, catalogs, and rates your website is called "crawling." Each search engine sends out "spiders" that periodically "crawl" over all the websites. They look for and record keywords contained in the website (such as in this case "florist," "Springfield," "MO"). So, when you enter those keywords in the browser search engine, they know what websites match what you are requesting.

The spiders not only crawl over the copy you can see, it also looks in places you can't see. It examines titles and labels like meta-tags or hidden index pages. These are important elements to have within your website so you gain SEO credit and thereby improve your organic placement higher in the list.

You can see the importance the development of your website has on your SEO rankings. If you build a website without good SEO elements, you're going to lose ranking position to competitors. And you really don't want to be below the top five.

Other ranking factors we know determine relevance are:

- The volume of traffic you have on your website. The search engines assume that if a lot of people visit you, you must be good.
- The age of the domain name and how long your domain name has been registered. You get credit for longevity.

These are just two of hundreds of considerations the search engines use to determine search results. There are no exact instructions provided; no one blue print to follow to tell you exactly what you need to do to be awarded the top positions. (If they did make this public, there would be no one in second place.)

Even if they did tell you all the exact rules today, they wouldn't be the same rules tomorrow... Google actually changes their algorithm rules more than 500 times per year.

How to Improve Your SEO

There are two areas of SEO you should focus on: On-Page SEO and Off-Page SEO

On-Page SEO

On-page SEO pertains to how you build your website. These are factors you can control such as content, keyword density, unique meta tags and page description data, search-friendly header tags, search friendly URLs, ALT tags, the coding of the website, the number of pages, etc.

Search engines look for these things and award more favorable position when they see that your website is "set up" right. A good website or

SEO manager who regularly tests your website and makes adjustments will improve your website's positioning.

Off-Page SEO

Off-page SEO includes many different factors as well. Here are some brief descriptions:

Link building—an over-simplified way to view links are when your company's name appears somewhere online other than on your own website. When the search engines see you appear in many places online, they view it like a popularity rating. They think you're more important—that there is more interest in you or your product/service. The future of link building is questionable because of its validity. Google's Penguin algorithms are attempting to discredit these links because they are built for volume, not for relevance.

Articles/blogs—creating your own content and getting other online sites to display or reference it creates more links. Submit your content to many of the top article directory sites.

Of course it helps if you're actually saying things that are relevant and useful. The goal is to inspire the readers to go to your website themselves or come right in and buy!

Online discussions—when you participate in forums or discussions you also build links, if you're allowed to have your username point back to your website. This is particularly beneficial when you're in niche forums or online communities.

There are many other methods used today, some far more advanced. I won't attempt to list more here because by the time this book is printed, something will have advanced on this subject. You must seek out what is currently working through an online search.

SEO improvement is ongoing

With this level of intense competition, you can easily conclude SEO is not a "set it and forget it" operation. Optimization requires regular testing, analysis and editing. Sit still and leave it alone will almost guarantee a quick decline.

It's important to note that SEO improvements often take time to kick in and move you up the list. If you do everything you should, it may still take months to significantly move your ranking up the line.

Directory Building

Directory building is also part of SEO. Directories are like websites that have a large listing of businesses.

There are thousands of directories online, many of which the average prospect will not use. However, there are currently approximately 20 generic directories that you should ensure your listing is included in because they will help your SEO.

Be careful investing in online directories. You need to find one with a significant amount of visitors each month—and don't be afraid to contact other businesses who advertise in them to see if they are seeing a return on their investment.

Some of the more successful directories are managed by television station websites. Those stations can have thousands of visitors a month, which can translate into a large number of Impressions and searches for your business. Calculate the cost of the ad compared to the number of views it will get each month to determine if the investment is worthwhile.

The more places your website has a link to it, the better your organic search results will be. Search engines consider you to be **more relevant** if other sites link to your site, but be careful—they have to be **valuable links**.

One old tactic employed by less-reputable SEM companies is called "link silos." SEM "experts" will build a phony website and start linking anything and everything on it—usually websites they are performing SEO and SEM for.

For example, Smith SEO has built a website for Mary's Flowers. Smith SEO then builds ten fake, one page websites where he just stashes links to Mary's Flowers. Mary now has ten links to her website, but they are on websites that have no traffic of their own or any value to a searcher.

Link silos will wind up hurting your search results in the long run because the algorithms used by the search engines now evaluate the sites where your links are built. So a television station website that gets 100,000 visitors every month that has a link to your website on it creates credibility and relevance for your website.

Online Advertising

There are many new online advertising methods being introduced every week. I'll discuss the most popular (as of this moment). You should look online to see others and the most current applications.

Pay-Per-Click Advertising

Pay-Per-Click advertising (PPC) is one of the most popular methods to improve your SERP (Search Engine Results Page) positioning when your "organic" placement is not high enough (i.e. you're not listed within the top five). You'll see PPC ads on search engines like Google or on social networking sites like Facebook. (This doesn't require you to set up a Facebook page. You can advertise on social platforms without having a page.)

Pay-Per-Click ads are set up just as they sound. You set a maximum bid. If you are the highest bidder at any particular moment, your ad will appear and you'll pay that bid amount every time someone clicks on it. The amount you pay is based upon a bidding process for "keywords" that can change in a fraction of a second. Certain categories and search terms are more expensive than others because they are in higher-demand (i.e. personal injury attorneys, car insurance).

You find most Pay-Per-Click ads on search engines along the very top and right hand side of the page. This "paid positioning" can help improve your organic search results if people are clicking on your ad. They drive traffic to your website, which increases your traffic, which can improve organic results.

Pay-Per-Click campaigns can be beneficial, but can also get very costly. However, underfunding will reduce your Frequency, and just as in traditional advertising, your results will probably decline.

If you are in a very competitive field (such as personal injury law) be prepared to invest some serious time and money. If your field is less competitive (and you have a good ad, a good landing page, etc.), you might get away with a few hundred dollars a month for some good results.

Display ads

Display ads include banners, pop ups, and videos that appear next to other content on websites. You can purchase banner ads on popular websites such as the local media websites, trade websites, social websites, etc. These are usually priced on a certain number of Impressions over a fixed period of time. The price is often referred to as Cost-Per-Impression or CPI for short. If you purchased AdWords it will be priced and displayed as CPM (Cost Per Thousand).

Display ads are being used more often in re-targeting strategies.

Advantages:

- Inexpensive to design
- Easy to measure
- Can increase interest and engagement if placed on a relevant page

Disadvantages:

- Often ignored
- Can be blocked

Online Video

Many, including myself, predict that in the next few years websites will look like television networks. People will soon get tired of reading about you and expect you or your spokesperson to entertain and educate them. Not much can entertain better than video.

Current studies show that websites with online video retain views 23 percent to 46 percent longer than websites without them. Just like with your brick and mortar location, the longer someone stays on your site, the more likely they are to buy something. So keeping them engaged longer increases your chance of converting the sale.

Technology has made it possible for the average person to make and edit a reasonably entertaining video that people will watch. YouTube has made grainy, amateur video mainstream and acceptable. You don't necessarily need the costly, higher quality production videos you would have just a couple of years ago. Don't get me wrong – better production still has its advantages, but now it's not the only option.

Here are a few good rules to follow:

- Don't just put up video for the sake of having video. If it doesn't do anything to enhance your credibility (like testimonial videos) or to explain your services, you are wasting the prospect's time.
- Don't always try to sell. Use video to inform and educate. You need to be sure they continue to evaluate. If you're the one providing content to help them, you'll probably be the natural choice to provide the solution if they move forward.
- Before you invest in a video for your website, ask yourself: "Who will care, and how does it benefit the prospect?"

- This said, if you are considering video, you need to discuss this with the web designer, because he or she will have to make room for video in the page layout. You don't want to have to go back in six months to do a re-design to make room for a video player.

Social Media

Another Disclaimer: By the time this book is in your hand, this section might already be out of date. Social marketing is currently the most-rapidly changing form of advertising; the rules and players change on a daily basis.

Social Media refers to the online interactions among people in which they create, share, and exchange information and ideas in virtual communities and networks. It is often people with similar interests who are researching, surfing, or just keeping up with friends and family. Social Media comes in many different forms including forums, magazines, blogs, social networks, music, photographs, video, etc.

Social Media's popularity continues to grow, with more people spending more time on social than any other type of site. From 2011 to 2012 the average time on social sites increased more than 33 percent. It can reach big audiences, as well as small ones, and it provides unprecedented measurement and control to the advertiser.

Commercial advertising had a slow start in online social circles. People felt that it was intruding into their personal lives and conversations. But hasn't advertising always done that? As it has grown, Social Media is demonstrating not only greater acceptance, but a powerful and persuasive force among groups, companies and individuals.

You can generate leads on social sites in many different ways. You can create or join Twitter lists that relate to your industry. You can join LinkedIn groups, establish your credibility and then approach potential customers or clients. You can share your latest video, blog or eBook on

Facebook. Google+ Hangout gives you the opportunity to connect in real time and put a face to your business. You can post tutorial videos on your own channel on YouTube. The options are seemingly endless. Each of these give you an opportunity to connect, get acquainted, discuss, learn, and teach with a number of different tools.

Social Media follows the trend discussed at the beginning of this book: Customers are no longer willing to be sold something; they want to discuss and learn before they make a commitment. Social marketing is certainly more in-step with that way of thinking than traditional advertising.

Social Conversion to Sales

Early social marketing conversion seemed to be more effective if you had a product or service that was "social" or fun. Social products and services that had higher sales conversions include:

- Candy
- Alcohol
- Major food brands
- TV shows
- Movies
- Music, bands
- Bars and restaurants

I had a client who ran a plumbing company. He was very serious about promoting his business on Facebook. It really didn't go very far. In fact, it tanked (no pun intended). I don't know about you, but I really don't want to see the latest toilet a plumber installed in someone's home. I also don't use a plumber very often, so I don't feel it necessary to follow him to get an instant coupon.

However, other customers may want to visit this plumber's Facebook page to look at the number of followers and reviews before calling. So, you can't discount doing the best you can with Facebook.

These days many doors have opened up for social applications within many types of businesses. Even dentist and physicians are able to create social communications that engage customers. The rule is basically whatever subject somebody would like to hold a discussion about or research, you may have a social marketing opportunity. Since Social Media is relatively inexpensive to operate, I suggest you learn more and try this yourself.

Be Careful Who You Let Post

A warning about social media: Just because you employ a 20-something staff member, does not mean they are a social media *marketing* expert. I drive a car, but that doesn't make me a mechanic. We have had to correct some really bad social posts placed by a client's employees.

Likewise, if you do use social media, do not give administrative rights to every employee. All it takes is one accidental post about "last weekend's party" to damage your business reputation online.

You also need to limit fan posts and feedback or remove it altogether unless you are going to monitor it around the clock. We have a very large client who sent a memo requiring "someone" create a Facebook page for the business. Six people took it upon themselves to create one. None knew about the others, and some allowed fan postings to their pages. One of the pages had profane messages railing against the client on the wall for ***more than two weeks.*** Since none of the online staff knew the page existed, they had no idea the reputation-blasting post was there for 20,000 fans to see. Ouch.

Social marketing takes time to learn and to gain results. You'll need to learn and test. I would recommend you create a social media plan and calendar that identifies your target, message, post frequency, goals and measurements for each social site. This will give better direction (and reminders) of what you're trying to do and how you're trying to do it.

Beyond that advice, social marketing is far too involved and is changing too rapidly to try to give you more in-depth understanding. My suggestion is to do what I do: Go online and learn how to use the latest and greatest applications of social marketing. There is more content for this online than you can imagine.

Reputation Management

This is a biggie. If you've got people talking bad about you online, you've got trouble. Studies show 80 percent of people will bypass and not consider a product, business or service that has a bad online review when other options are available to them. They just don't want to take the risk.

This is a very dangerous situation. Businesses currently have little control over what people (or competitors) write about them online. I've personally seen this cause significant reduction in inquiries, website visits and referrals, regardless of their validity. You just can't defend yourself as well as you should be able to.

There are new and emerging software and online services that try to assist you with this. Most, simply keep an eye out online to alert you whenever they find your name being drug through the dirt. Others use tactics to try to "bury" the reviews by promoting other customers (and whoever) to write good reviews.

When you see negative reviews, it is critical you respond to them immediately. A quick response shows that a business truly cares about what customers say and demonstrates they try to create a satisfactory conclusion or compromise.

This is an area that is going to grow in importance, but don't wait to get some sort of reputation management system for your business.

7

PUBLIC RELATIONS

Another component of marketing is Public Relations (PR). PR is not a form of advertising. Advertising is paid; PR is most often free.

Another fundamental difference is that with advertising, you can control content and run as much and as often as you like. With PR, you can submit your story, but someone else controls if it runs and the final content. Often the media will run their own story and there is little to nothing you can do about it.

The biggest advantage of PR over Advertising is that with advertising, people know you're spinning the message to sell or convince. PR has greater credibility because the content is provided by an unbiased, third-party. When you can get it, good PR often outperforms paid advertising.

PR is more restrictive and often requires an established relationship with traditional media outlets to ensure more frequent publication. It can be time consuming, and even if you have a great newsworthy story, you can always be replaced by "breaking news." If you into rely on PR as a substantial part of your marketing, plan to invest a large part of your time building media relationships, or find yourself a firm that specializes in PR and already has the connections.

8

PLANNING

Normally you would expect to see a book like this begin with Planning. I felt it was more important to put it toward the end, after you became aware and understood all the options you have and issues you must consider.

Since I don't know your business, I can't help you lay out a plan. But I can give you some tips on how you can do it for yourself.

Your first step is to create a written plan. I find for most, this is much easier when they use a business planning software program.

You will also need to consider how to "administer" your plan on a daily basis. I'll tell you about some ways to handle that as well.

Business/Marketing Planning Software

A written plan is very important because it keeps you, your project and your company focused and on track. It is a collaborative document that keeps everyone "on one sheet of music."

Earlier in "Building a Brand" I discussed a planning process that requires a substantial amount of information, objectives, assignments, timelines, etc. This is all too much data and communications to track in emails or on yellow tablets. Formulating a written plan, and how it works and how it's shared, merits discussion.

Most small business owners and manager create their plans in programs like Word. While this can work, I have always disliked it due to the indexing issue.

When creating a business brand development and/or marketing plan, it is well worth the money to invest in a specialized software program. There are several good options available and most are very affordable. I prefer committing my plans to Palo Alto software (Google them).

These types of software programs give you a good starting format and the flexibility to customize it to your specific needs. They even automatically re-index when you make changes (this alone is worth the money). There are new versions that you can share online. Most have change email notifications, administrative protections that allow viewing, and comments without editing permissions, etc. It will take little time to master the software, but it's far better than a word processing program for this type of task.

Task and Timeline Tracking Programs

While I recommend you use these programs to assemble your written plan, they can be a little difficult to use as a daily reference or checklist to keep you on track. I typically start with a narrative format plan that carries all the details, history, logic, etc. Then I convert as much as I can down to a "task with timeline" level and track it on Microsoft Project 2010. This gives me an immediate critical path tool that will keep me on time and on track since it operates on a critical-path basis.

Project-Level Collaboration Programs

Two programs I like for project level collaboration are Basecamp and Dropbox. Basecamp has several features such as discussions, file up-

Planning

loads, comments, text documents, and even a To-Do List. For a place to simply upload and share documents or large files, I prefer Dropbox. Check them both out online.

Keeping Track of the Plan

I'll be the first to admit that it's one thing to create a great plan, but quite another to keep track of all the things you're trying to accomplish. Sometimes the sheer volume or complication of an operational or marketing plan can be overwhelming. This is why I recommend you copy the task onto line items using Excel or consider learning how to use Microsoft Project 2010.

Trying to use a yellow note pad to work your marketing program can prove to be difficult. Using a program like Excel or Microsoft Project make the tasks easy to read, adjust and assign. You can also use it to track your marketing budget efficiently.

9

POST-PLACEMENT EVALUATION

Post-placement is based on both measureable results and indicators. It is the science of accessing what actually happened.

After all the pre-placement planning of Impressions, Reach and Frequency, GRPs and such, now you have to figure out if it actually worked.

Some media results are easier to assess than others. For instance, you can run a coupon ad in a magazine. When buyers walk through the door and hand you the coupon, you know it worked.

Most other traditional media applications are much harder to measure effect. Normally your only options are to measure them based on indications. Indication measurement is the process of trying to determine the effectiveness of any given media based on variations, trends and patterns. Look for variations in calls, store traffic or sales within the time period you start and stop the media.

Online offers a good way to measure traditional media using your website traffic as your indicator. Many people go to websites to research a product or service they've become interested in. If you've successfully created awareness through the media, you should notice a discernible variation in the number of visits. You may also notice more "likes" on your company Facebook or LinkedIn company profile page. This gives you a good indicator.

External and Internal Performance Factors

Unfortunately, there are countless variables that can contribute to the success or failure of your advertising efforts. They are **External Factors** or **Internal Factors.**

Before you can determine the success or failure of your advertising, you will have to fairly and honestly consider what impact these factors had on your sales volumes. Make no mistake, this is difficult to do. Just use common sense, refrain from emotional influences, wishing or exaggeration, look beyond the obvious, and you'll probably arrive at a more accurate conclusion than you would by simply ignoring them.

External Factors

- Weather
- A recession or high unemployment
- War
- Holidays
- New competition or other promotions
- Bad product or service publicity
- Your business (or personal) reputation
- Road construction
- Etc., etc., etc.

Your marketing and advertising may be doing exactly what it was designed to do. Under normal circumstances, you should be able to see some predictable results. However, any one (or more) of the factors listed above could substantially change the outcome. And too often, they do.

Post-Placement Evaluation

Hidden Results

Sometimes your advertising could be doing a great job, but you may not even see it.

For instance, I had a client who constantly remarked that his advertising "had no effect whatsoever" on his bottom line during a recession. After asking the client to compare his competitor's sales to his, he found that they all had a minimum of 20 percent loss in sales (YOY). If he had not done his homework, he would have killed an advertising program that was actually rewarding him with a 20 percent sales lift!

I will often tell my clients, if you think your advertising isn't working, turn it off and see what happens. This is sometimes risky, particularly with high competition. If they lose that top of mind awareness, it can send their advertising efforts back to square one. It's healthy and vital for you to question the results of your advertising, but can be risky to knee-jerk and simply turn it off because you "feel" or "think" it isn't working.

On the other hand, it's just as bad to keep writing checks to the media if you're not sure it is paying for itself. So I think that if you can, you should, but just be prepared to reinstate if you find your business drops off.

Do your homework. Compare year-over-year and month-over-month numbers to assess your sales, profit and loss, and ROI. You might find your advertising is doing better than you thought.

Internal Factors

As I said earlier, if you have internal issues, it is difficult to isolate and measure the exact contribution of an advertisement or marketing program. Until you assess and improve your brand position, you'll never really know how well you're doing or could be doing.

A thorough SWOT (Strengths, Weaknesses, Opportunities, Threats) analysis can help you identify some internal factors you might not otherwise consider to be affecting your business. Though it might seem tedious, or almost silly, you have to consider things like your phone number, answering service, and company name as potential internal factors that can affect sales. If your widget store phone number is similar to your competitor's, you could be losing sales to sloppy dialing. If your company's name creates an unfortunate web address (Lake Tahoe's Board of Tourism website "Go Tahoe" creates this questionable URL www.gotahoe.com), you could be losing clients. Don't discount the importance of looking at every aspect of your business.

Isolate Your Media for Measurement

Consideration must be given to variable conditions that occur during promotional periods, i.e. seasonal demand, severe weather, political/ economic environment, local or national crises, etc.

If you do this with good discipline, you should be able to see some indications of movement. Often the variations will start small and not appear to justify the expense. But overtime with consistency it can gain momentum until you may even take it for granted.

Sourcing the Cause

Sometimes the wrong media or marketing effort gets the credit for what another did. Yellow pages were notorious for grabbing the credit from other advertising for decades. People would see a print ad, billboard, TV ad or hear something on the radio that compelled them to purchase. They would go to The Yellow Pages to get the phone number or address.

Then, when they called or visited the store and were asked, *"what brought you in?"* They would cite the last thing they used: The Yellow Pages directory. This is why The Yellow Pages were able to command such outrageous prices for their ads. They were getting credit as the procuring cause of the purchase for way too long.

For many years I've helped telemarketing companies like Wyndham attract new recruitment prospects. This is a high turn-over labor pool often staffed by college students. For years, we've found that television is the very best media to use for this job. We can demonstrate people in a fun, high-energy environment with testimonials and such.

I recently ran a blitz campaign for Hank, a long-time friend who owns a successful telemarketing firm. When I asked if it was delivering enough new prospects he replied, *"Not really, but it always amazes me how the help wanted sign I've had out front forever seems to immediately become far more effective when I run my television ads."*

You Must Continually Test

The effectiveness of media is changing radically. Audiences are becoming fragmented. More and more I hear business owners say, *"What worked in the past doesn't work anymore."* This is why, more than ever, you must continually test your media to know you're investing your money the right way.

You must also remember to give each media adequate time to perform. Don't knee jerk! Any media should be given between 60 to 90 days to demonstrate it can create awareness.

Measurement Is Not Without Flaws

Much of today's advertising and marketing training materials advocate measuring the prospect count in your store to determine if your advertising is effective. This is not easy to do. It takes extraordinary discipline to remember to inquire what brought in each and every new prospect. Unless each and every new prospect is identified and tabulated, it is rarely accurate enough to compare to a quantifiable measurement.

Marketing Survival in a Digital World

As marketers, we face a double-edge sword with all the new measurement methods—we love providing clients with numbers and statistics to show results. We really like to see the successes—and failures—as much as you do.

The problem is, not every medium is easy to measure, and now that we can measure about 60 percent of what we place, the other 40 percent that is "un-measurable" starts to feel "un-justifiable" to the advertiser. Don't fall into this mode of thinking. Just because I can't assign an exact number of customers who came in from your TV ad (through prospect measurement), that doesn't mean it didn't factor into their A.I.E.A.A. decision-making process. Your TV ad might not have been the last thing they saw before they decided to come in, but it might have triggered the thought process that caused them to investigate you online. That buyer's A.I.E.A.A. might have looked like this:

Awareness: Radio ad for Ted's Widgets—*"That's the third time I've heard that ad this week. Wonder who they are."*

Interest: *"Darn, I broke my widget and now I need a new one. I think I heard a commercial on the way to work about that. Let me think of who that might be."*

Evaluation: TV ad for Ted's Widgets—*"Oh, that's the ad I heard on the radio the other day. Let me go to Ted's website and see what they charge and where they are."*

Acceptance: *"I have to fix that widget today. Ted's got some good reviews on that customer review website, so I think I will use them. Their price is in my range, too."*

Action: *"I am calling Ted's to buy that widget. Let me get their phone number from the phone book. Hello, Ted's Widgets?"*

Okay, over simplified, but this is actually pretty typical of how we make buying decisions. Look at how many media channels played a role in this scenario—radio, TV, website, referral sites/directories, and the phone book. If you ask the customer, *"Where did you hear about us?"* How do you accurately track that? Which media gets credit for the sale?

Do you know what answer you will get most often? *"The phone book."* In reality, the phone book is simply the last place they looked to get your phone number. They have been influenced on some level by all of your advertising efforts, just at different stages along the way.

So, while you can confidently track an online sale to the website as the main source of influence, you need to keep in mind that the buyer had to first learn you have a website, what the address is, and that you carry the product they need. Coupons, tracking codes and separate phone numbers can often help you identify a large portion of your revenue. Keep this in mind when you are using tracking methods to source your sales.

The bottom line: Financial measurement far surpasses prospect measurement in terms of accuracy in ROI. Tracking and new technology have made it easier to measure the effectiveness of your advertising, but for now, you won't be able to track 100 percent. Mass media response is harder to source than single media, but a good advertising campaign will use more than one vehicle for delivering a message.

Technology Makes It Easier To Measure

The future looks much brighter for eliminating the guesswork in advertising. New technology is providing incredible analytical and reporting advances for advertising and marketing. Most of it is available for free!

On Facebook you can measure "Likes" as an indication of interest in your company, product or service. With Twitter you can do the same with the number of "Followers" you have.

As I stated before, Google provides a free program for you to measure activity on your website. Google Analytics can disclose a wealth of information regarding the activities and interest of your website visitors. You can track:

- Total visitors, where they came from (geographically and from referring sites), how long they stayed
- The number of pages viewed, how long they stayed on each page, which pages were most and least popular
- What areas of your pages are clicked through most and least
- Pay-Per-Click ad performance
- Integrates with certain email marketing programs to track how many people visited your website by clicking on an email

These are only a few of the many reporting features available on Google Analytics. If you want or need to know information about your web traffic, you **must** install this on your website. The most important thing to remember is that the information can be used to help you determine how your other advertising efforts are working. Web traffic isn't the entire story, but it is an invaluable tool for helping to evaluate shopping and buying habits of your customers.

For Email effective measurement, services like Mail Chimp, Constant Contact, iContact and others used today come with reporting features that allow you to view the number of opens, click-throughs, bounces, etc., from the emails you send, down to identifying which email address clicked on which link.

Regarding Email, let me stress this: the important thing is not simply to look at open and click rates and say "ooh" or "oh no." You need to consider your goals for each email you send. Do you want people to go to your website to learn more, or do you really just want them to print the coupon and come in to your store? The numbers themselves are great, but you need to use them to determine who is an active purchaser, who is just browsing, and who is not really in the market for your goods. From there, you can use the data to focus on your hot and warm leads, but continue to

Post-Placement Evaluation

just "drip" reminders on others who might not be ready to buy, but because of our thin market concept, might be in your market in the future.

10

MARKETING & ADVERTISING AGENCIES

I found out years ago I had a real talent for losing money in the stock market. I bought some investment software and thought I'd soon be lying in the sun on Tortola, laptop on my lap and earning great wealth as a day trader.

After a dabble with it and when it was all tallied, I realized I should have just gone to Las Vegas and put it on the table. I learned that I needed to do something to put the odds in my favor. I concluded I needed to enlist the help of a professional financial gambler who knew when to hold them and when to fold them, and when to let the stock split. I needed a professional financial planner.

A financial planner or broker does not have a crystal ball and can't guarantee anything. However, they put the odds in my favor to win through their experience in the financial field. My investments have made more money than I expected even after paying their fees.

This same value holds true with marketing firms or advertising agencies. As a former marketing director, I employed advertising agencies. I now own an agency. So, I have some insight that might help.

Whether you're a big or small business, you can—and should—investigate working with a reputable advertising agency or professional. The additional expense you'll incur will most often be minimal compared to the money you'll potentially lose making mistakes on your own.

Advertising agencies come in all sizes, from working out of their spare bedroom to Madison Avenue high-rises. Although most tout themselves as a "full-service agency," most actually work in one of several primary areas:

- Research
- Graphic design
- Audio/video production
- Media planning/placement
- Web design & development
- Consulting
- Public relations
- SEM & social media

Full-Service Agencies

A true full-service agency might do all of these services. One advantage of working with a full-service agency is that they can often provide better brand growth and maintenance because it's all handled in-house. Another advantage to a full-service agency is that their clients may receive more honest and un-biased counseling because the agencies services are not limited to any single media they must sell to generate income (i.e. video, graphics). More solutions can be freely recommended because the full-service agency will be paid either way.

On the other hand, you may pay more for services at a full-service than you might at a smaller Boutique or Specialty agency.

Boutique or Specialty Agencies

Small or specialized boutique marketing agencies may offer services at a lower price and/or with greater value due to expertise and efficiency in their given field. For these same reasons, more full-service agencies are now employing free-lance or special service agencies as their client's needs become more diverse.

Employing an Agency

Marketing and advertising agencies are paid several ways: retainer, hourly fees, by project, per media placement, etc. An agency can even be in-house, meaning they work exclusively for one firm.

Your business should certainly consider working with an advertising agency if your advertising volume is substantial. Planning, adjusting and running large on-going multimedia promotions can be very distracting from your normal business tasks, and should be left to the advertising professionals.

Take the time to investigate agencies. Ask your colleagues in business about agencies they have dealt with or have heard about. Interview a few until you find the right fit.

Oftentimes, if two or three agencies have similar quality work, chemistry and personality will help you make a final decision. Nobody wants a working relationship that will be strained from the start.

Once you have seen samples of their work and have some testimonials from other clients, choosing an agency should be a fairly painless task.

CONCLUSION

I underestimated how difficult it would be to write this book. During the five years I've been trying to put it together, marketing and advertising has been changing so rapidly that much of what I wrote became outdated before I finished. Still, most of the content and principles should be useful for some time to come.

My hope is that this book will help small businesses understand how to market themselves more effectively and competitively. To help them avoid wasting profits on un-tested marketing advice from those who publish content more to promote their personal SERP position than to share useful information. To learn how good marketing practices and application can help them improve their business and improve their relationships with their customers.

Small business is critical for our survival. As populations increase and job opportunities decrease due to technology, where is this leading us? Entrepreneurs and small businesses offer the best hope of employment for our children and grandchildren. We should all support more small businesses for their sake.

Made in the USA
Charleston, SC
26 October 2013